HENRY COUNTY
TENNESSEE

Will Abstracts
(Vol. 1 *and* 2)

- 1777-1820 -

Compiled by:
Lela C. Adams

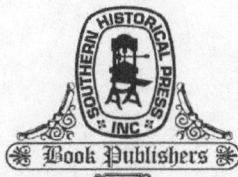

Southern Historical Press, Inc.
Greenville, South Carolina

Please direct all correspondence and orders to:

www.southernhistoricalpress.com
or
SOUTHERN HISTORICAL PRESS, Inc.
PO BOX 1267
Greenville, SC   29601
southernhistoricalpress@gmail.com

ISBN #0-89308-544-8

Printed in the United States of America

PREFACE

Henry County is located in the south western section of the Piedmont along the North Carolina line. It was formed in 1776 from Pittsylvania County and originally included all of present day Patrick County and that part of Franklin County which lies south of the Blackwater River.

Henry County was named for the Revolutionary War patriot and orator Patrick Henry. Patrick Henry lived here from June 1779 to December 1784 and represented the county in the House of Delegates during his residence.

These two will books cover the period of 1777 thru August 1820. Will Book I contains 306 pages and covers Feb 1777-1799; number II 1799-1820 and is 353 pages in length. The Wills are not necessarily in year sequence, apparently accumulating and enteres into record at various times without regard to dates.

All proper names have been included in the index with the exception of the slaves. These have been omitted due to the repetition of names in the Will, then Inventory and in some Sales.
Most of the Inventories indicate pounds, shillings and pence only the later ones using dollars and cents.

Lela C. Adams
Sherwood Forest
Bassett, VA 24055
September 1984

I:1 Inv. & Appr. ZEBULON SHELTON 17 Feb 1777 by Josiah Smith, Joseph Sowal, Hugh Armstrong..horses and saddle T:75.12.6.

I:2 LWT IZRAREAL TURNER 18 Feb 1777
To be buried at the discretion of the Commanding Officer of Ft. Patrick Henry. To older brother half the value of negro Bob all clothing in the possession of David Chadwell in Pittsylvania County on Smith River, wages due from the Commonwealth and also to my brother JOHN. To my half-brother WILLIAM TURNER a cow and calf. Wit: G.Hartt ?, John Redd.

I:2-3 LWT JAMES WILSON,SR. 1 Apr 1777 Prb: 21 July 1777. Wife MARTHA WILSON to have use of negros Sarah, Seal and Adam; son THOMAS to receive negros Sarah and Seal at mother's death and son MOSES to have Adam. At death of Martha daus MARTHA BALEY and ANN BROSHEARS to have money resulting from the sale of the plantation. Exors wife and two sons.
Wit: Toliver Cox, Russell Cox, Joseph Goodwin. Sec. for exors John Blagg, Toliver Cox.

I:4 Inv. & Appr. SILVANUS WEBB 12 Feb 1777 Retd: 21 July 1777 by Robert Chandler, Micajah Pool, Nathan Hall..includes horses, cattle, saddle, tomahawk, books, bond and accounts due from Thomas Barksdale, Samuel Johnson and Julius Scruggs. T:46.17.0. James Rea, Admn.

I:5 Inv. JAMES WILSON SR. 1 Aug 1777 Retd: 18 Aug 1777. Cattle, sheep, furniture, tools, 3 negros T:247.10.0.

I:6 LWT WILLIAM COOK of Bedford County 4 Mar 1776 Pr. 16 Sept 1777. Brother JOHN COOK, if he returns from the War to have a horse or to the child his wife is expecting. Father, JOHN COOK, to dispose of the estate to his brothers and sisters (not named) and to be exor.
Wit: William Dunn, John Bohannon, Joshua Bohannon.

I:7 LWT ROBERT HILL 31 July 1777 Pr: 16 March 1778. Wife VILOTE and six children..daus: RUTH, MARY, JOHANAH, HANNAH. sons: SWINFIELD and THOMAS. Sons to be exors.
Wit: Benjamin Roberts, James Standefer, Adam (x) Barns. Sec: for exor Peter Saunders, James Martin.

I:8 LWT JOHN FRANCE -Nuncupative Will.10 Feb 1778 Pr: 18 May 1778. Sons: PETER, HENRY, DANIEL, HAMON and JOHN. Daus ELIZABETH and SARAH. Wife MARY. Negros Milly, Solomon, Sylvia, Rose and Fanny. Exor: Hamon Critz Jr and Thomas Smith. Their sec.

1

Archelaus Hughes.

I:9 Nuncupative WILL ABNER HARBOUR 18 Mar 1778.
Mildred Moore and Judith Riddle appeared before
Edmund Lyne J.P. and made oath that about the 2nd of
May last they heard ABNER HARBOUR dec'd in his last
sickness desire his estate to be divided among his
children..land to his four sons: DAVID, MOSES,
ELISHA and THOMAS, balance of estate amongst all his
children.
Ret'd by JOYCE HARBOUR, widow and relict of Abner
Harbour, who was appointed Admn with Phillip Anglin
and John Witt her sec.

I:9-10 Inv. & Appr. NATHAN COCKRUM 20 July 1778.
Dishes, furniture, hogs, saddle, horse, bible,
cattle..no total by Humphrey Scoggin, Thomas
Edwards, Waters Dunn.

I:10-11 LWT JOSEPH ROBERTS 27 May 1778 Pr: 17 Aug
1778. Land whereon he now lives, 520 ac, to three
sons: JOHN, JOSEPH and JAMES. James is the
youngest. Wife ELIZABETH ROBERTS to have
possession during her lifetime. Dau NANCY ROBERTS
to have money when she comes of age. Rest of the
estate to be divided between his wife and his four
children. Exor Thomas Jones and James Spencer.
Wit: Thomas Lowe and James Roberts. Sec. for exors
James East, Leonard Vandergriff, Arch. Hughes.

I:11 Inv. ABNER HARBOUR 15 Aug 1778 by George
Rowland, Thomas Jamison, Benjamin (x) Moor..includes
cattle, sheep, horses, hoggs, tools, gun, pewter and
furniture. no T.

I:11 Inv. JOHN FRANCE 22 June 1778 Retd: 17 Aug
1778 by Hamon Critz Sr, John Parr, Richard
Adams...includes horses, cattle, furniture, 5 negros
T: 685.13.6

I:13 Inv. ROBERT HILL 21 Aug 1778 by William Cook,
James Standefer, Benjamin Griffith..cattle, sheep,
furniture, horses, law book,bible, tools. T: 393.1.6

I:14 Inv. JOSEPH ROBERTS 12 Sept 1778 Retd 21 Sept
1778. By: Arch. Hughes, Frederick Fulkerson, George
Taylor...one negro Tom, a copper still, horses,
cattle, tools, furniture.T:995.13.

I:16 Inv. MOSES HARRIS 25 Mar 1779 by George
Waller, John Briscoe, Elisha Walling...2 negros,
cattle, horses, looking glass, cooper's tools, gun,
hunting saddle, furniture...T:1286.0.0

I:17 LWT MERRY WEBB,SR,sick and weak..6 Feb 1774

Pr: 15 Feb 1779.Wife ELIZABETH WEBB to have negros
Robin, Peter and Jane and estate for life. Son JOHN
WEBB to have negro Joe; son MERRY WEBB to have negro
Hannah;dau MARY BURNS negro Lewis; dau ELIZABETH
SAMS negro Ben; dau LUCY WEBB negros Sarah and
Aggy..son MARTIN WEBB, daus MARTHA DILLARD and
MILLION HALL.Exors sons MERRY WEBB and JOHN WEBB
and wife ELIZABETH WEBB. Wit: Will. Tunstall,
George Elliott, John (x) Ray. Sec. for exors Waters
Dunn, Philip Ryan, John Alexander.

I:18 Inv. & Appr. estate of JACOB LINDSAY,dec'd by
Frederick Fulkerson, James Spencer and John Dillard.
29 Jan 1779 Retd: 15 Feb 1779. negros:
George,Charles,Joe,Nell,Nancy,Breechers,John, Bobb,
Ben,Will, Nann, Jane and children, Aggy, Lucy.
Horses, wagon, cattle, sheep, furniture, cherry desk
and table, tea table, decanter, surveyors
instruments, money scales, books, sword, gun.
T:6762.19.6.

I:20-21 Inv & Appr estate of SAMUEL JONES,dec'd 13
Sept 1777..by Esaias Harbour, Mathew Small, Joel
Harbour..cattle, horse, furniture, working tools
T:26.1.6
15 Feb 1779 sales to: Peter Hairston, Esaias
Harbour, John Jones Sr, Henry Chiles, John Newman,
James Denny, George Jones.

I:22 Inv estate of NICHOLAS LANGFORD
27 MAY 1779 By John Cameron and Joseph (x)
Cameron..cattle, horses, furniture ..T:30.2.0

I:22-23 LWT LILYAN HAMPTON,sick and weak...14 Apr
1779 Pr 27 May 1779. Legatees: son JOHN RUSSELL,
his dau SUSANNAH RUSSELL, son SAMUEL PARKER,dau
LILLYAN FLEWD. Cash due from William Bowman and
David Right. Exor. Deveraux Gilliam, Thomas
Stockton. Wit: Deveraux Gilliam, Elizabeth
Hutchison, Edward Gilliam. Sec for exors James
East.

I:23-24 LWT LEONARD TARRENT 3 July 1777 Retd 27
May 1779. To wife MARY TARRENT estate during her
lifetime or widowhood..six children: LARKIN
TARRENT,REUBEN TARRENT, CARTER TARRENT, WINIFRED
TARRENT, TERRY TARRENT, RACHEL TARRENT. Exors
Leonard Tarrent Sr, Richard Tarrent, son Larkin
Tarrent.
Wit: Will. Tunstall, George Tankersly, Jemima
(x)Miller.
Mary Tarrent Admn with sec Richard Tankersley, James
Tarrent, Leonard Tarrent.

3

I:24-25 Inv & Appr estate LEONARD TARRENT, JR. 6
June 1779 Retd 27 Aug 1779. Horses, cattle, sheep,
hogs, furniture, 3 negros, sugar box, 4 vol.
Josephus' works, 2 bibles, prayer book,geese,bee
hives. No T. Ret'd by John Blagg, John Burch,
Marvel Nash.

I:26 Inv estate JAMES COOK 10 Apr 1779 Pr 26 Aug
1779. By: John Farguson, Swinfield Hill, Thomas
Hill, Edward Choate..5 negros, Dick, Dedum, Bob,
woman and child; furniture, cattle, etc..T:3358.0.6

I:27 Inv estate WILLIAM DABNEY 2 June 1779 Pr 26
Aug 1779. By: Peter Gilliam, Thomas Heard, John
Heard.....cattle, horses, furniture, 1 negro,
plantation tools..no T.

I:28-29 LWT JOHN GOODE, sick and weak, 16 May
1779 Pr 26 Aug 1779.
Wife, FRANCES GOODE. children: WILLIAM GOODE, SARY
GOODE, JOHN GOODE, MARTHA GOODE, JESSE GOODE, NANCY
GOODE, THOMAS GOODE. Exors William Hunter and Thomas
Cooper.
Wit: William Heard, William Estes, John Heard.
Sec. for Exor: Willaim Estes, William Heard.

I: 29-30 LWT JACOB GOLDEN,weak in body.. 17 Sept
1779 Pr: 28 Oct 1779.
Wife MARY GOLDEN. Son WILLIAM GOLDEN..if unborn
child is a male to share in estate with
William..daus not named. Exors Thomas Stockton,
Richard Dickens.
Wit; Joseph Sowel, John Bender, Thomas (x)Jones.
Sec for exors Thomas Adams and James Shelton.

I:30-31 LWT THOMAS GIBSON 3 Jan 1780 Pr 30 Mar
1780.
Wife MARY GIBSON, dau CUZZIAH GIBSON. Exor
Zackeriah King, Joel Gibson, Lambert Dodson.
Wit: Charles (x) More, Joseph (x)Nichols, William
(x)Moore.
Lambert Dodson and Champane Gibson sec for Joel
Gibson.

I:31 Inv & Appr JACOB GOLDING 11Mar 1780 Retd 23 Mar
1780
By John Cameron, William Taylor, John Dillard,
includes hogs, sheep, horse, cattle, furniture, gun
and tomahawk for a T:1584.4.4.

I:32 Inv & Appr SETH FLOOD 25 May 1780
By James Dickinson, William Halbert, John
Grisim..cattle,sheep, hogs, gun and farming tools
T:176.14

I:33-34 Inv & Appr JOSEPH CAMMERON 25 July 1780 Retd
27 July 1780.
By William Taylor,John Marr, Josiah Smith..horses,
cattle, wagon, copper still, furniture, farming
tools T:11,692.0.

I:34 Inv & Appr THOMAS GIBSON 27 Apr 1780
By   Philip   Anglin,   Daniel   Goldsby,   Lambert
Dodson..livestock,   farming   tools,   household
furniture...no T.

I:35   Acct   Estate   of   JAMES   HICKS   by David
Lanier,Admn.
Pd Clerk of Pittsylvania Co, Field & McCall, John
Colley, clothing items for Miles Hicks and Nancy
Hicks; expenses 182.12.9, income from hire and sale
of one negro 430.8.6.

I:36 28 Sept 1780, the guardians to the orphans of
JAMES   HICKS dec'd to Alexander Joyce..material,
stockings, shoes for orphans..due John Calley; for
boarding Miles Hicks 6 mos; Nancy Hicks 3 mos;
Elizabeth Hicks 13 mos and to board 4 children for
17 mos. Negro sold to John Wagnon??.

I:37 LWT JOHN ROWLAND 6 July 1780 Pr 29 Sept 1780.
To my brother MICHAEL ROWLAND'S eldest son WILLIAM
ROWLAND a cow and calf and to his brother MICHAEL
ROWLAND 1 shilling.   To my brother GEORGE ROWLAND
land I got of George Lumkin on Marrowbone Creek. To
John Palfree land where he now lives and clothing.
To my wife MARY ROWLAND money, if she abides by this
Will.   To Obedience Ryan, wife of Philip Ryan, a
negro named Phillis; to GEORGE ROWLAND JR   and
WILLIAM ROWLAND,sons of GILBERT ROWLAND,1/6 part of
the net; to the two sons of JOSHUA BOWLS,dec'd one
hundred pounds for their education with their mother
SARAH BOWLS as trustee.

To GARLAND AIKEN when he becomes 21 yrs of age
one-half of the estate.   A deed to JOHN WELLS is to
be executed, being 280 ac on Leatherwood Crk sold
him, land conveyed to me by Paul Carrington. George
Rowland, Jr is to act as Clerk of the estate. To
MARY ISHAM,wife of JAMES ISHAM, 2 cows. Appoint
William Tunstall, Haynes Morgan, Peter Saunders and
Josiah Carter exors. I appoint Patrick Henry, John
Fontaine and John Salmon to receive profits arising
from the estate, also be guardian and trustee for
Garland Akin.
Wit: Baldwin Rowland, Henry (x) Barksdale, John
Salmon.
Sec for exors William Tunstall and Peter Saunders
are George Hairston and John Fontaine.

I:39 LWT JOSEPH EARLY, in an ill state of health..Washington Iron Works 22 July 1780 Pr 23 Nov 1780.
To brothers JOHN EARLY and JUBAL EARLY all of my estate..but will expect them to do something for my brother JEREMIAH EARLY if alive. Uncle Joshua Early to make the division between my brothers John and Jubal and act in my stead with James Callaway for my brothers and sisters.
Wit: Bartlett Wade, Fo... ...,Thomas Keepers.
Admn. John Early with George Hairston and James Spencer sec.

I:40-41 Inv & Appr JOHN ROWLAND, SR. 26 Oct 1780 Retd 23 Nov 1780. By Mordecai Hord, Henry (x) Barksdale, Brice Martin...horses, wagon, cattle, other livestock, rye, books, furniture and 6 negros,Alice, Betty, Will, Hampton, Blacksmith, Jacob. T:529.2.0

I:42-43 Inv & Appr estate MERRY WEBB 1 Aug 1779 Retd 23 Nov 1780.
3 negros, Robin, Peter, Jane; household furniture, livestock..T:1932.13.0. By Joseph Anthony,John Fontaine, Jacob Riegor ?.

I:43 Inv & App estate THOMAS GARNER 2 Dec 1779 Retd 24 Nov 1780. By Peter Hairston, Spencer Reynolds, John Wells. Household furniture, farming equipment, livestock. T:1146.10.0.

I:43-44 LWT JOHN BLAGG 22 Feb 1781 Prb 22 March 1781. To godson WILLIAM TUNSTALL son of WILLIAM TUNSTALL negros Jube, Patrick, Obediah and woman Frank, should he die before of age to PEYTON RANDOLPH TUNSTALL, son of WILLIAM TUNSTALL. To THOMAS BARKER TUNSTALL a sorrell mare. To god daughter MARY DICKINSON dau of THOMPSON DICKINSON a cow and calf. To WILLIAM TUNSTALL, father of my god son, my riding horse, saddle and bridle. To my niece MARY WATTS the residue of the estate. Should she die her part to be divided equally between RICHARD WATT'S children, the children of MRS. MC HARG, late wife of ALEXANDER MC HARG. Overseer Thompson Dickinson to remain. Appoint William Tunstall, Richard Watts, Nicholas Darnell and Mary Watts exors.
Wit: James (x) Melton, Fred. Rehm, Thomas (x)East, John (x)Kendrick.
John Salmon, A. Hughes, Henry Lyne sur for William Tunstall.

I:46 LWT WILLIAM EAST in a low state of health..1 Feb 1781 Pr 22 Mar 1781.

6

To brother JOHN EAST clothing..to JOHN EAST JR second son of my brother John East, a colt; to MICAJAH BAYS a colt; to wife SARAH EAST livestock and balance of the estate. Appoint Micajah Poole and James Stratton exors.
Wit:John Mackoy, John East, James Rea,Jr.
Admn Micajah Poole's sec William Graves and Henry Lyne.

I:47-48 Inv & Appr estate GRIMES HALKUM 10 Aug 1781 Retd 22 Nov 1781 by John Woods, Hugh Woods, Hugh Martin..horses, cattle, hogs, tools, furniture..T:25,028.0.0

I:48-49 Inv & Appr estate WILLIAM LETCHER 25 Nov 1780 Retd 24 Jan 1782 by James Armstrong, William Mitchell, William Hudspeth. 9 negros, Nann, Sook, Abraham, Witt, Dick, David, Ben, Randolph, Craft,livestock, horses, house furniture. no T.

I:49-50 LWT PETER TURLEY, in a low state of health..6 Oct 1781 Pr 28 Feb 1782.
To oldest son WILLIAM TURLEY 5 pounds.Wife SARAH TURLEY. to youngest sons LEONARD TURLEY and SAMUEL TURLEY the estate at Sarah's death or marriage. Appoints wife Sarah Turley and son-in-law Owen Hunt exors.
Wit: Peter Smith, Spencer Clack, Benjamin Chandler.
Sec for exors: Peter Smith and Benjamin Cook.

I:50 Inv & Appr estate of WILLIAM EAST 1 Dec 1781 Retd 28 Feb 1782.
By Waters Dunn, John Alexander, James Rea. Bond on John McCoy, livestock, furniture. T:277.17.6.

I:51 LWT JAMES TURPIN 13 Sept 1779 Pr 28 Feb 1782.
Wife MARGARET TURPIN to have use of the estate her lifetime or remarriage then to go to the children(not named)..appoints Henry Jones and Robert Jones,Jr. exors.
Wit: William Cook

I:52 LWT ISAAC JONES 9 Mar 1781 Pr 28 Feb 1782
Wife RACHEL JONES to have a horse, furniture, the price of 2/3 of a tract of land patented in the name of Henry Jones being 152 ac. Land where I now live to my son ISAAC JONES. My wife may be pregnant, if a son, Isaac to give him 20 pounds. Daus MILLA JONES, RACHEL JONES, ELIZABETH JONES, HANNAH JONES, SARAH JONES and SUSANNAH JONES. Wife, Rachel Jones to be exor.
Wit: John Kelly, John Rentfro, Joel Walker.
Sur for Rachel Jones; Joshua Rentfro and John

Rentfro.

I:52-53 LWT JOHN PINKARD,yoeman, 7 Jan 1782 Pr 28
Feb 1782.
To wife JANE PINKARD estate for life, then to
children (all underage), JAMES PINKARD, ELIZABETH
PINKARD, JOHN PINKARD, CHARLOTTE PINKARD, JANE
PINKARD and THOMAS PINKARD. The land is to go to
JAMES PINKARD and JOHN PINKARD. Appoint wife Jane
Pinkard and brother Charles Pinkard exors.
Wit: Peter Smith, Dinah (x) Littrell
Sec for exors Hugh Innes, Daniel Richardson, Spencer
Clack.

I:54-55 LWT ELISHA ESTES 13 Jan 1782 Pr 28 Feb
1782.
To son ELISHA ESTES 2 negros David and Gran; to son
JOEL ESTES 2 negros Joseph and Fanny and land; to
son AMBROSE ESTES negros George and Jude; to dau
SARAH HUTCHINSON negro Febe; to son ABRAHAM ESTES
negros Daniel and Joseph; to son WILLIAM ESTES
negros Dick and Robin; to dau BARBARY HOLT negro
Anthony; to dau ELIZABETH EVANS negros Sarah and
Sam; to dau MARY NIGHT negros Rose and a boy; to son
RICHARD ESTES negros Philip, Bristat?,Hannah,
Peter; to ELISHA HOLT, son of BARBARA HOLT and
AMBROSE HOLT. To wife MARY ESTES the use of the
plantation and use of 7 negros: John, Peter, Jesse,
Tom, Fanny, Nan and Grace. Dau RACHEL ESTES in care
of her Mother, and is to have 3 negros for her
support, at the death of her Mother, Richard or Joel
to take care of Rachel. Appoint sons ELISHA ESTES
and RICHARD ESTES exors.
Wit: William Choice, Joshua (x) Townsend.
Sur for exors: Samuel Patterson, John Davis, Eusebus
Hubbard.

I:56 LWT JOHN RAMSEY, sick of body..3 Nov 1781 Pr no
Wife MARY RAMSEY to have use of the plantation where
he now lives and a tract of 113 ac during her
widowhood..small children..SAMUEL WEBB to have
right and title to 100 ac whereon he now lives. The
six sons are to receive the property at mothers
decease, namely: GEORGE RAMSEY, JOHN RAMSEY,
RANDOLPH RAMSEY, THOMAS RAMSEY, JAMES RAMSEY and
WILLIAM RAMSEY. Exors John Dickerson, Edward
Richards.
Wit: John Dickenson, Edward Richards, Eliza
Richards.

I:57 Inv & Appr ELISHA ESTES 25 Apr 1782
by Daniel Richardson, William Ryan, Spencer Clack.
14 negros: John, Peter, Nann, Fann, Grace, Tom,
Jesse, Robert, George, Tony, Buster, Hanner, Joseph,
Febey, house furnishings, livestock, plantation

tools.

I:58-59 Inv & Appr ISAAC JONES 23 May 1782. By Thomas Jones, Peter Gearheart, Robert Jones..cattle, furniture, tools, books..T:77.16.4.

I:59-60 Inv & Appr ANDREW KELLY 20 Apr 1782 Retd 23 May 1782. By Shadrack Woodson, Stephen Lee, Joseph Showers Price..T:51.6.0.

I:61 LWT ISHAM HODDGES 14 Mar 1782 Pr 23 May 1782. When the youngest child becomes 21 yrs of age, 600 ac to be sold. Eleven children: WILLIAM; ISHAM, MOSES, ROBERT, AARON, ASA, dau AMNIJAH ??,JUDA, KEZIZAH, MARTHA and NANCY. Aaron and Asa are the eldest sons. Appoints Frederick Rives, Robert Hoddges, John Dickerson Exors. Wit: Fred. Rives, John Price, Abednegoe Hoddges. Sur for Robert Hoddges are Robert Masson and William Heard.

I:62 Inv & Appr ISHAM HODGES 15 1 June 1782 Retd 17 June 1782 by Frederick Rives, Samuel Patterson, Edward Richards. No T.

I:63 Inv & Appr JOHN PINKARD 27 June 1782 by William Ryan, Arthur Edwards, James Majors and Abel Edwards. Negros: Roger, Sall, Jean, Kit, Bob, Joe, Jude, Denmark, Peg, Moll, Rachel, Peter, Hanner, Moses, Ned, walnut desk, wagon, livestock, house furniture, tools..no T.

I:64 Inv & Appr JOHN RAMSEY 13 July 1782 Retd 25 July 1782 by William Heard, Robert Hodges, William Manning for a T: 36.16.9.

I:65 Estate acct of WILLIAM DABNEY dec'd to Anny Dabney admn 2 June 1779. Pd Jesse Heard; James Finley, William Swanson, James Spencer, John Stewart, William Taylor, Jesse Dilling, Andrew Rea, Richard Peremon, Hickerson Grubbs, George Heard, William Haynes, Lewis Jenkins, John Hartwell, William Heard and John Cox for various accts and supplies T:1,185.9.0 Received of Patrick Lockhart and James Harris and others T:3,230.19.7. By James Cowden, George Heard, Baines Holloway.

I:66 Inv & Appr PETER TURLEY 23 July 1782 Retd 26 Sept 1782 by Hugh Innes, Arthur Edwards for a total of 42.1.9.

I:66-67 Inv & Appr JACOB TROUP 4 APR 1782 By Thomas Jones, Sr; Robert Jones, Owen Rubell..horses,

cattle, sheep, hogs, geese, furniture, tools
T:113.0.1. John Huff made oath 4 Apr 1782 that Jacob
Troup indebted to him for the first colt from the
gray mare.
Due from Margaret Turpin to the estate of Jacob
Troup dec'd 112.10 paper currency due two years last
March.
The estate of Jacob Troup dec'd I have not sold but
kept in my possession and have maintained the
children out of the profits. signed Mary Troup,
Admn.

15 Aug 1782 Paid John Huff one colt in full against
the estate of Jacob Troup dec'd. 26 Sept 1782.

I:68-69 1770 - Estate of THOMAS DAWSON in account
with John Carter exor..item: removing estate from
N.C. to Pittsylvania Co. Va. Item: Charles Carter's
execution from Goochland Co. Pd James and Robert
Donalds stores. Pd David Bridges in part of the
widows legacy.

I:69-70 Acct Estate of THOMAS DAWSON in account with
Josiah Carter Exor.
Orphans, Martha Dawson, Betsy(Betty); Susannah and
Martin Dawson.
Pd Clerk of Amherst; bacon from James Jackson; pd
Edmond Winston attorney fees; pd William Mitchell
attorney fees; pd acct at Goochland store, to James
Bluford for selling negros; pd Col. Williams atty in
suit against John Grymes, pd Dr. Cabell; pd Henry
Innes; Anthony Bitting for a hunting saddle for
Martha Dawson and one for Susannah Dawson..hire of
negros to John Rowland and Josiah Carter; cash of
David Bridges for John Grimes.
signed: John Salmon, George Waller, Goerge Hairston.

I:72 Inv & Appr RICHARD NOWLAND 24 Oct 1782 by Peter
Gilliam, Isham Blankenship, Jr; Henry Lester. No
total.

I:72 LWT THOMAS NELSON, sick and weak,..18 Mar 1782
Pr 28 Nov 1782.
Wife SALLY NELSON..children not named..Appoints wife
Sally Nelson exor with Morris Webb and James Ray.
Wit: S. Sampson, Marey (x) Mark?, Dorothy (x)
Morris.
Admn of estate sec are Waters Dunn, Thomas Prunty,
James May.

I:73 Inv & appr estate THOMAS NELSON Nov 1782 by
Joseph Anthony,Sr, Joseph Farguson, John
Bricoe...furniture and some items in the hands of
William Swanson.

10

I:74 Inv & Appr goods of THOMAS WATTS,dec'd in the hands of Edward Richards by John Martin, Joshua Dillingham, Robert Mason. 22 Apr 1783 T:3.2.6.

I:74 Inv & Appr JOSEPH EARLY 24 Apr 1783 By: John Doughten, Mordecai Modsley, Swinfield Hill..bar iron, tobacco, clothing, gun, cattle T:1063.3.4.

I:75 Appr goods and personal estate of JACOB KOGER 13 June 1783 by Charles Foster, Anthony Tittle, Samuel Allen..horses, cattle, one still, furniture, hogs T:79.19.9. Retd 26 June 1783.

I:76 Inv & Appr estate ABEL BETTY 26 June 1783 by Robert Mason, Thomas Hill, Hugh Woods. ..negros: Delf and child; Sam, Ben, Keat and 2 children and other items T:342.13.0.

I:76-77 Estate acct of JOHN ROWLAND in acct with Peter Saunders Retd 25 July 1783.
Pd items for Garland delv'd to Thomas Nunn. Pd Col. Williams; pd George Carrington, pd Mordecai Hord, Col. Tunstall, suit of George Rowland, suit of James Spencer.
Receipts from: William Graves, Edward Baker, Benjamin Dillen, Dr. Reid, John Lackey and Josiah Carter.

I:78 Inv & Appr estate of WILLIAM KELLY 23 Aug 1783 Retd 28 Aug 1783 for a total of 4.16.0 by George Sumpter, John Briant, Samuel Packwood.

I-79 Inv & Appr estate WILLIAM MARTIN 25 Sept 1783 by William Adams, James Ingram, Anthony Tittle..no total.

I:80 LWT JAMES SPENCER, JR..sick of body..21 Sept 1783 Pr 29 Nov 1783.
Wife MARGARET SPENCER use of land on Horsepasture Crk till JOHN comes of age 21 yrs, use of negros: Matt and wife Loosey, Loose and Ned. Two oldest sons are JOHN SPENCER and WILLIAM SPENCER to have land. Four children namely, JOHN SPENCER, WILLIAM SPENCER, JAMES SPENCER, GEORGE WASHINGTON SPENCER. Aged father and mother to have the plantation on which they live for life. Give to father, mother, brothers and sisters all twenty pounds. To Uncle Thomas Stone, his wife and children twenty pounds each. The land on Marrowbone Crk for benefit of two youngest sons, James and George Washington. The house now building to be covered and future expense from the account of John and William. Appoints John Dillard, James Shelton and John Stone exors.
Wit: Thomas Stone, John Stone.

Sec for exors: Abraham Penn, A. Hughes, Brice Martin.

I:81 Inv & Appr estate BENJAMIN COOK 27 Feb 1783 by William Ryan, Hugh Innes, Spencer Clack...includes negros Ben, Siller, Charity, Nan, Nance, Jude, Mary, Fann, Doll and 3 not named, horses, wagon, gun and saddle..no T.

I:82-83 Inv & Appr estate JAMES SPENCER 10 Jan 1784 Retd 22 Jan 1784 by Josiah Smith, Joseph Morris, Samuel Morris..10 negros, horses, cattle, sheep, hogs, hemp, furniture and farming tools. No T.

I:83 Inv & Appr estate JOSEPH ADAMS 27 Nov 1783 by Hamon Critz, Thomas Smith, Peter France..horses, cattle..T 26.10.0.

I:84 Estate Acct of JAMES HICKS with Alexander Joyce guardian Retd 25 March 1784..Board and clothing items for 5 children..Income from hire of negros Andrew, Taz, Amy and Ben's boy.

I:85 LWT JOHN WATSON, being sick and weak..30 Oct 1783 Pr 25 Mar 1784.Legatees: dau ELIZABETH WATSON to have negro Nell; son ALEXANDER WATSON to have negro Sill; to dau EDEY WATSON negro Nan; to son JAMES WATSON negro Pegg; to dau MARTHA WATSON negro Sis. The rest of the estate to be divided among the whole of my children. Exors to be James Watson and Hawood Masshire?.
Wit: Zackariah Prather, William Spencer, Benjamin (x) Griffith.

I:85-87 Acct Current estate of ISHAM HODGES, dec'd with William Ryan. Retd 25 Mar 1784.
Accts: William Haskins, Daniel Richardson, James Stewart, David Woodall, Samuel Baird, Joseph Channell, William Hodges, John Cook, John Keen, Robert Lang??, William Cowden, Moses Hodges, Isham Hale, John Dickenson, William Bartee, Janson Brown, John Kerby, Jesse Hall, William Graves, Abednigo Hodges, Jeremiah Channel, Robert Hodges, David Kerby, John Martin, William Jamison, William Hodges, Isham Hodges, Isham Hall, Littlebury Laws, William Ryan, Stephen Hodges. Acct of Robert Hodges against estate of Isham Hodges. Accts of Daniel Richardson, Edward Richardson, Samuel Beard, John Price, John Dickenson, John Keen, Abraham Bendeventer, Joseph Blair and John Chandler.
I:87-88 Estate accounts of ISHAM HODGES,dec'd 25 Mar 1784.
To Robert Hodges, acct Edward Richards, John Cox, James Prunty, John Price, Stephen Hodges, 5 days in

Montgomery County.
I-88-89 Acct of ISHAM HODGES, dec'd 25 Mar 1784.
Accts of Frederick Reeves, Robert Woods, Joseph
Blair, John Martin, Robert Large.

I:89 Inv & Appr estate JOSEPH PERSONS 10 Dec 1783
by George Reynolds, William Stevens..a horse, saddle
and clothing T 15.11.0. Retd 22 Apr 1784.

I:89 Inv & Appr estate JEREMIAH POOR 30 Apr 1784
Retd 27 May 1784 Admn. William Ferguson.
Cash 6.0; a proved acct against the estate of Joseph
Rentfro 2.15.6.

I:90-91 LWT SHADRACK TURNER 25 Oct 1783 Pr 22 July
1784.
To sons LARKIN TURNER and JEREMIAH TURNER the
plantation where I now live as far as a branch, a
horse and saddle to each. Son WILLIAM TURNER land,
joins Daniel Smith and the wagon ford. Dau EXONEY
TURNER land on Turkey Pen Branch and horse, saddle
and livestock. The balance of land to sons LARKIN
TURNER and JEREMIAH TURNER. The house is to be
finished out of the estate. To wife ANN TURNER
plantation and stock for life then to be divided
among all my children and grandaughter ELIZABETH,
JOHN, JOSIAH, WILLIAM, MARY, LARKIN, JEREMIAH,
EXONEY, and MARY HUNTER. Sons John Turner and
William Turner to be exors.
At marriage LUCIA ROBBS to have a cow and calf, but
if Lucia or Sally die without issue, to return to
estate.
Wit: Samuel Crutchfield, John Hunter, Richard (x)
Stone.
Sec. for exors: Peter Saunders and Robert Stockton.

I:91 LWT WILLIAM STANLEY, very sick..17 Aug 1784 Pr
28 Oct 1784.
Wife JUDY STANLEY to have estate during her
lifetime and at her death grandson WILLIAM STANLEY
is to have a horse, then the balance of the estate
to be equally divided among all my children: MARY
STANLEY, JOHN STANLEY, WILLIAM STANLEY, MOSES
STANLEY, RICHARD STANLEY, HANNER ROBERT STANLEY,
JESSE STANLEY, JANE MULLINGS, JUDY BUCK, ANN ATKINS.
Exors to be wife Judy Stanley and son Richard
Stanley.
Wit: John Turner, William Hunter, William Mullings.
Exors Judith Stanley and Richard Stanley sec George
Rives and William Mullings.

I:92 Inv & Appr estate THOMAS PUCKETT 27 Oct 1784
by Ralph Shelton, Rod. Moore, John Daniel. Eliphaz
Shelton, Admn. Mare, saddle, skins T.22.1.5.
In the hands of the Admn Eliphaz Shelton is cash and

paper dollars and a militia ticket.

I:93-94 Inv & Appr estate JOHN BLAGG 24 Aug 1781
Retd 26 Nov 1784 by Richard Tankersley, John
Tarrent, Richard Daniel. Includes 13 negros: Abram,
Jack, Jacob, Jesse, Nann, Esther, Sally, Sophia,
Prue, Frank, Jua, Patrick and Obediah, furniture,
family bible, 3 vols Stanhopes Works upon the
Gospel, prayer book, black walnut desk, stock,
plantation tools. No T.

I:95-96 LWT HENRY HAYNES 5 Mar 1784 Pr 23 Dec
1784.
To son WILLIAM HAYNES negro Willoby. To son JOHN
HAYNES the one hundred pounds that he is indebted to
me and a cow and calf. To dau DINAH ENGLISH negro
Barnaby and at her decease to her son HENRY ENGLISH.
To my son HENRY HAYNES negro Violet and child Febe
and the 200 ac where he now lives. To my dau MARY
GREER negro Frank. To my son PARMENAS land on
Craddox Crk and negro Sam and a horse. To dau ANN
GREER negro Booker. To granddaughter MARY ANN
GREER bed, cow and calf.
Appoint sons George Haynes and Parmenas Haynes as
exors.
Wit: Phillip Realey, John Clarkson, Joseph (x)
Clarkson.
Sec for Henry Haynes and Permenas Haynes are John
Rentfro and William Greer.

I:96-97 LWT JOHN HICKEY not dated Pr 23 Dec 1784.
To wife MARY HICKEY plantation, mill, stock and
furniture for life then to sons to be equally
divided between them. To son JAMES HICKEY land on
Beaver Crk begins at Samuel Gardner's line; to son
JOSEPH HICKEY land at the head of Horsepasture Crk;
to son JOHN HICKEY 400 ac on Ramsey Crk; to son
BENAJMIN HICKEY land on Rock Run Crk on the south
side of Smith River; to son CORNELIUS HICKEY land
on Rock Run Crk; to son ELIJAH HICKEY land on Morgan
Bryan Rd beginning where Daniel Smith's path goes
into; to son MICHAEL HICKEY land on Rockcastle Crk;
to dau MARY HICKEY land on Warp Mtn Crk and Grassy
Fork; to dau JANE HEARD land on the little fork of
Reed Crk; to dau NANCY HICKEY land on the middle
fork of the Grassy Fork of Buttram Town Crk.
Mary Hickey and William Heard Jr executors.
Wit: John Goode, John Cunningham, Rhoda (x)
Dillingham.
Sec for exors: Thomas Nunn, Thomas Prunty.

I:98 Accts of estate of JOHN GOODE, dec'd with
Thomas Cooper executor. Retd 25 Sept 1784.
8 Oct 1770 Pd to Abraham Penn 262.7.6.
29 May 1782 to William Hunter, a land warrant

purchased for the estate 1050.0.0.
25 Jan 1781 to the widow,.Frances Goode 205.0.0,200. and 50.
To Solloman Jordon 1/8 part of his acct.
Receipts dated 1780-1783 from John Cooper, Joseph Cooper, John Dillingham, William Kitchen, Grymes Holcomb, Jacob McCraw, Molley Hickey, Blakey and Maupin, Joseph King.

I:99 Acct of JOSEPH CAMMERON 10 Dec 1784 Retd 24 Feb 1785.
Pd John Pullum as per acct of John Cammeron; pd Thomas Hambleton; pd acct of Susannah Cammeron; pd Surveyors.
Examined by A. Penn, John Marr, John Dillard. We have divided the estate of JOSEPH CAMMERON between the widow and 8 children, each childs part 12.12.6 and widow 50.8.6.

I:100-101 LWT JAMES SHELTON, sick and weak in body..14 May 1784 Pr 26 Mar 1785
To wife PHILEPINEA SHELTON plantation for lifetime or until my sons NATHAN SHELTON and JAMES SHELTON come of age; use of five negros: Grace, Kike, Jack, Abraham, Cate. Balance of estate to be divided between my five children: NATHAN, JAMES, MOLLY, NANCY and SALLY. If my wife is with child, to be made equal with the others. Appoint my son William Shelton, Archealus Hughes and John Salmon exors.
Wit: John Watson, Christopher Owens, Jacob Stallings.
Sec for exors: George Hairston and John Dillard.

I:101 Inv & Appr estate WILLIAM STANDLEY 26 May 1785 by John Turner, William Turner and John Hunter..livestock, furniture, horses, guns..T: 58.4.3.

I:102-103 Inv & Appr estate JAMES SHELTON 13 May 1785 Retd 28 July 1785 by William Taylor, Joseph Morris and Samuel C. Morris..5 negros, furniture, livestock..T:397.8.0.

I:103-104 Inv & Appr estate HENRY HAYNES 10 Jan 1785 Retd 25 Aug 1785 by William Swanson, Philip Realy and David Clarkson...8 negros:Violet and children; Buker, Sam, Pegg, Barnes, Wittabe and Frank, household furniture, tools, horses..T: 493.7.3.

I: 105-107 Acct of Sales estate HENRY HAYNES 16 Jan 1785.
To: Parmenas Haynes, Robert Cowan, George Haynes, William Swanson, David Clarkson, William Burdet, Henry Haynes, Jeremiah Maxey, John Haynes, Henry

English, Philip Realy, Capt. Benjamin Green and Stephen Hail..T:67.10.11.

Acct HENRY HAYNES 16 Dec 1785 Retd 22 Sept 1785 payments to: Clerk of Henry Co.,2 coffins Philip Realy; Thomas Hunter acct; William Haynes, Parmeneas Haynes, exor. T: 70.5.11.

Receipts from: Philip Realy, Henry English, Henry Haynes Jr, Capt. Parmeneas Haynes, William Swanson, David Clarkson, George Haynes, Jeremiah Maxey, William Burdett, John Haynes, Stephen Law, Benjamin Green, Stephen Hail and Robert Cowan.

I:107-116 Acct JACOB LINDSAY, John Lindsay and Sarah Lindsay Admn. Retd 1 Oct 1785.
Oct 1776 - 1785
Pd Timothy Hatchatt, William Miller and Peter Scales for schooling children; to Jacob Stalling for cutting out negros close; Thomas Miller for fees; Edmond Winston, Col. Henry Bell, William Powell, Ralph Eldridge; Clerk of Buckingham Co; Capt. Thomas Miller, Edmond Wilcox, Col. A. Hughes; John Staples, Rachel Gouge, William Hugins dancing master; to Henry France for board at the dancing school; William Taylor.

Pd Spencer's executors for Mrs. Sarah Lindsay who gave an order to Thomas Scott for sundries; Samuel Anderson for surveyors fee; hire of John Lankister, hire of William Gray, John Patterson, Charles Owen; trip to Buckingham and Caroline counties and to Richmond; pd Maj. John Dillard (formerly of Amherst Co); pd Edmund and Henry Lyne; pd Jarrott Patterson and James Lindsay two of the legatees of James Lindsay dec'd of Caroline; to Col. George Hairston, Miles Hicks, Mr. Marr, Col. Hughes; pd Henry France for board of Ruben and William Lindsay to go to school; pd Mr. Golladay for teaching Carroline and Ruben Lindsay dancing.
Receipts from: Thomas Smith who was undersheriff to Jacob Lindsay; from Stephen and Bird Smith exors of Guy Smith, dec'd; from Jacob Cox exor of William Powell dec'd by hands of Thomas Miller, from James Shelton, John Marr. No T.

I:117-118 LWT TULLY CHOICE, weak of body..2 Nov 1777 Pr 27 Oct 1785.
To dau ELIZABETH HALL, wife of William Hall, 5 shillings, received hers previously; to dau ABE BOLLING, wife of Samuel Bolling, 5 shillings; to son TULLY CHOICE, land; to son WILLIAM CHOICE land on Snow Crk; to son JOHN CHOICE 200 ac land (under 21yrs); son CYRUS CHOICE land (under 21yrs); dau SOPHIA CHOICE (under age); dau SUSANNAH CHOICE; dau MARY CHOICE; wife to have negros and stock. Exors

16

to be sons Tully Choice, William Choice and Samuel
Bolling.
Wit: William Hunter, William Estes, John Richardson.
Sec for exor Tully Choice, William Ryan and Benjamin
Cook.

I:118-119 Inv. part of the estate of JOSEPH JONES
30 Aug 1785 Retd 27 Cot 1785 by Swinfield Hill, Luke
Standefer, William William Menefee, Stephen Smith.

I:119-120 LWT PETER DAVID 21 Dec 1781 Pr 25 Nov
1785.
The following children have received their portion:
PETER DAVID, JUDE DAVID, JENEY RALEY and ISAAC
DAVID. Three eldest daus ANNA DAVID, ELIZABETH DAVID
and MARY DAVID after death of their mother to
receive bed and furniture, cow and calf and two
sheep. To two youngest daus MAGDALENE DAVID and
PHEBE DAVID bed, cow and calf and sheep. To son
ABRAHAM DAVID land on Big Bull Run. The balance of
the estate to be equally divided among all the
children at the death of their mother ELIZABETH
DAVID, who is to have the use of the estate during
her lifetime or widowhood. Appoints wife Elizabeth
David, Isaac David and Peter David exors.
Wit: George Haynes, William Greer, David Clarkson.

I:120-122 LWT JOSEPH ANTHONY 24 Sept 1785 Pr 22
Dec 1785.
To wife ELIZABETH ANTHONY during her life lend 9
negros:Cooper, Charcole, Matt, David, Ben, Lou,
Jude, Jean and Jean. Children: SARAH COOPER;
CHRISTOPHER ANTHONY, ELIZABETH CANDLER, PENELOPHY
JOHNSON, JOSEPH ANTHONY, JAMES ANTHONY, MARY CARTER,
AGNES BLAKY, these children received their part when
they married. To son MICAJAH ANTHONY land purchased
of James Young and 2 negros Milly and child. To dau
RACHEL ANTHONY 2 negros, Henry and Lucy. To dau
WINIFORD ANTHONY negros Charles and Sarah. To son
MARK ANTHONY land, negros Molly and Tim. To son
BOLING ANTHONY land and negros James and a child of
Milly which I formerly lent to James Johnson, now I
give to Micajah Anthony. To my dau JUDITH ANTHONY
negros Nan, David and child. If Penelopy Johnson
refuses to keep the negros as slaves, they are to be
returned to the estate.
Appoint as exors wife and sons Joseph, James and
Micajah and Thomas Cooper.
Wit: John Stokes, Ambrose Jones, William Jones, John
Jones.

I:122 Inv & Appr estate of JOSEPH ANTHONY 25 Jan
1786, by John Stokes, Jacob Ferris, Ambrose Jones
and William Whittells??.
Bonds, 19 negros, cattle, plantation tools, one

17

still, sheep, horses..No T.

I:125 Accts of the estate of JOHN ROWLAND with
Peter Saunders, exor.
Pd Col. Hairston, Clerk of Buckingham Co; Col.
Tunstall, Thomas Nunn for schooling Garland (Akin);
Pittsylvania Co; Abraham Penn.
Receipts from: Edward Baker, Waters Dunn Sr.

I:126 LWT LEMUELL LANIER 29 Jan 1785 Pr 23 Mar
1786.
To son WASHINGTON LANIER land and negro Luis. To
dau NANCY ARMSTRONG 2 negros Amy and Joy. To son
BENJAMILE LANIER negro Jack and land when he
becomes 20 yrs of age. To wife ELIZABETH LANIER
lifetime use of plantation at her decease to be
equally divided among all my children, namely: DAVID
LANIER, MOLLEY KING, SALLEY WILLIAMS, NANCY
ARMSTRONG, WASHINGTON LANIER and BENJAMILE LANIER.
Appoints wife and sons James Armstrong and
Washington Lanier exors.
Wit: John (x) Kichen, James Taylor, Elizabeth (x)
Kichen.
Sec for Admns James Armstrong and Elizabeth Lanier:
James Lyon, A. Penn, John Staples.

I:127-128 Estate Acct of THOMAS LOW by Joseph
Roberts 24 Mar 1786.
1778-1783 Received of William Taylor, Robert Baker,
William Roberts, Henry Grogan, A. Smith, A. Thomas.
Payments to: Thomas Hoff, E. Young, F. Fulkerson,
Thomas Baltcher, R. Roberts, Henry Grogan, James
Fox, Peter Scales, George Taylor.

I:128-129 Accts estate of ELISHA ESTES with Elisha
Estes exor.
Accts from Richard Estes of NC.

I:129-130 Accts of estate of JOSEPH JONES.
Pd John Rentfro sec for Joseph Jones; Thomas
Brandon, Peter Saunders, William Standefer, Nicholas
Alley, Daniel Spangler, Swinfield Hill.
Received of: John Bates, Jeremiah Bohanon, John
Fuson, John Huff, William McCoy, Alexander
Sutherland, Ebenezer Pyat, Jesse Rentfro, Peter
Saunders. William Standefer, admn.

I:131-132 Inv & Appr estate LEMUEL LANIER 27 July
1786 by Josias Shaw, James Taylor, Thomas Stovall.
Negros Toney, Agey, Nann, Peter, Jack, Ester,
Charles, Jim, livestock, tools. T: 473.8.5.

I:133-135 LWT BLACKMORE HUGHES, very sick and
weak....2 Aug 1786 Pr 24 Aug 1786.
To son JOHN HUGHES negro Jack; to son BLACKMORE

18

HUGHES negro Lucy; to son GEORGE HUGHES negro
Milly; to dau MARY ABSTON negro Hanner; to dau
ELIZABETH PRATT 30 pounds; to dau MARTHA HUGHES
negro Rose; to son ROBERT HUGHES 300 ac land on
Buffalo Crk lines of William Gardner, William Isam,
Robert Pilson and Butterworth. To dau SARAH
LAWRENCE 300 ac on Dols Crk. To wife ANN HUGHES lend
negro Sarah during her lifetime and after her death
Sarah goes to son THOMAS HUGHES. To son MOSES
HUGHES 70 ac land on Smith River; to son BEVERIDGE
HUGHES 100 ac land on Buffalo Crk.
Appoints wife Ann Hughes, friend William Amos and
son John Hughes admn..
100 ac at White Falls on Smith River to be
sold..some children underage.
Wit: James Morrison, Rebeckah (x) Morrison, Nancy
(x) Morrison.
Sec for exors: Nathan Hall, Adam Lackey, John
Henderson and William Isam.

I:135-137 LWT ROBERT MITCHELL 19 Apr 1786 Pr 28·
Sept 1786
Lend to my wife AGNES MITCHELL during her natural
lifetime personal estate, furniture, household items
and negros:Dunn, James, Luce, Hanner and Susana. To
son JOHN MITCHELL negros Frank and Sam. To son
WILLIAM MITCHELL negro Edward; to son GEORGE
MITCHELL negro Peter; to son RICHARD MITCHELL
negros Sarry and Allan; to dau JUDA COLLAR negros
Ben and Hannes; to dau AGGA BOATMAN one shilling; to
dau ANN POLLARD one shilling. After the death of
my wife, granddaughter AGGA BOATMAN to have a
feather bed, cow and calf. To my son WILLIAM
MITCHELL lend a negro during his lifetime, then to
his son JOHN MITCHELL. At the decease of wife, son
RICHARD MITCHELL to have negro Susanna and
furniture; dau JUDA COLLAR to have a looking
glass..the balance of the estate then to be sold and
divided between my sons JOHN, WILLAM and RICHARD
MITCHELL.
Exors: sons John Mitchell and Richard Mitchell.
Wit: Ignatious Simms, William Brown, John Haley.
Sec. for exors: Robert Stockton.

I:137 Accts. estate of THOMAS NELSON 28 Sept 1786.
To George Eleet, Joseph Farguson, John Smith, Ab.
Paine, William Swanson.
Adm. Waters Dunn.

I:138-141 Accts estate BENJAMIN COOK 26 Oct 1786.
Accts from 1778-1786. Pd Joseph Cook, James Cook,
admn, Aaron Mackanger, Tully Choice, Acct of James
Haggard, Daniel Baugh, Henry Innis, William
Whitlock, Abel Edwards, schooling children, Tulley
Choice Jr, Samuel Calland..sundries purchased at

Petersburg for the estate; pd for curing negros of
veneroal desease; pd acct William Jameson, Loucy
Richardson; traveling to Broad River, S.C. twice;
traveling to Cumberland Co.
Rec'd of Thomas Threlkeld, Jarrol Watkins, Richard
Gwinn, James Dillard.
Signed: Hugh Innis, William Ryan, Charles Pinkard.

I:141 Franklin Co Va..an order from Henry Co
directing us the subscribers to settle and adjust
the acct of Benjamin Cook, deceased with the admn
Benjamin Cook. 19 May 1786, signed: Hugh Innis,
William Ryan, Charles Pinkard.
I:141 - Acct of increase of the estate of Benjamin
Cook Retd 26 Oct 1786.. 3 negros, one bond,
tobacco, wheat, oats, corn. T 93.0.0. Signed: Hugh
Innis, William Ryan, Spencer Clack.
I:142 Report of Benjamin Cook's widows
dower..alloting her two slaves Nancy age 20 and Juda
aged 12 yrs. Dated 1 Sept 1786 Rtd 26 Oct 1786 by
Joel Estes, William Ryan, Charles Pinkard.

I:142-143 At a Court held for Henry County 4 March
1785..David Perryman, plantiff against Jesse
Heard..in de....a dark bay horse. Dismissed.
Defendant to recover his cost.

I:143-144 Inv & Appr estate JOHN GOODE Retd 27 Jan
1785 by Ambrose Jones, John Cooper..horses,
livestock, furniture, tools..No T.

I:145 LWT JOHN BROCK 8 June 1784 Pr 25 Sept 1784
To wife SALLY BROCK horse, cow and furniture; to
brother SHERAD BROCK cow and her increase due me
from James Bolling; father JOHN BROCK.
Exors: wife Sally Brock and brother Sherad Brock.
Wit: John Minter, Allen Brock, Jeams Malting.
Sur for exors: Samuel Tarrent and John Minter.

I:146 Inv est BLACKMORE HUGHES 9 Apr 1787 by
Thomas Morrow, Francis Turner, Mathew Small and
Joseph Herd first sworn by me Adam Lackey Justice of
Henry Co.
Tools, 6 negros, books, livestock, debts due from
Blackmore Hughes to Peter Saunders, Samuel Hairston,
Mr. Richmond, William McAlexander, Mathew Small,
John Henderson, Francis Turner, John Ingram, James
Ingram, Gideon Smith, Samuel Manin, John James,
Joseph Cogar.
Debts due B. Hughes by Samuel Noe, John Henderson,
Richard Pilson, James Elkins, William B. Price,
Barnabus Brannum.

I:148 Inv & Appr estate JOHN SWANSON 10 Apr 1787 by
William Graves Sr, John Alexander, John

Briscoe..horses, furniture..T: 51.8.9.

I:149 Inv & Appr ROBERT MITCHELL 1 Mar 787 Retd 10
Apr 1787 by James Armstrong, Richard Stockton,
William Brown..negros James, Susanna, 3
children..T:268.6.0

I:150 Inv & Appr RICHARD HOLT 17 Mar 1787 Retd 10
Apr 1787 by Mildred Holt, admn.
Household furniture, livestock..T 70.9.8

I:151 LWT HENRY MAYZE, sick and weak..4 Nov 1786
Pr 15 May 1787.
To son ABRAHAM MAYZE five shillings; to son SHERWOOD
MAYZE one shilling three pence; to son LITTLEBERY
MAYZE wheat; to son HENRY MAYZE a cow; to son DAVID
MAYZE land where I now live, 110 ac, horse, stock
and to take care of my wife PHEBY MAYZE; to son
GOODING MAYZE saddle and saddle bags; to son LIGGIN
MAYZE 120 acs that I purchased of George Lumpkin,
colt, feather bed and furniture; to dau ELIZABETH
GOSSET one shilling; to dau SUSANNAH HOLLANDSWORTH
five shillings; to dau FANNY SOLLAMON a small pot;
to dau PHEBEY MAYZE bed, furniture, dishes and
cotton and flax wheels.
Exors: David Mayze and friend David Lanier.
Wit: Alexander Joyce, D. Lanier, Joseph (x)
Chandler.
Sec for exors:John Staples, Nathan Hall.

I:153 Inv & Appr estate JOHN HICKEY 26 May 1785
Furniture, horse, tools T:25.5.6

I:153-154 Acct Orphans of JAMES HICKS by Alexander
Joyce.
1782 purchase of saddle, cloth, boarding 5
children.
Hired out negros Andrew, Tas, Amy and Ben.

I:154 Nansey Hicks orphan of JAMES HICKS to D.
Lanier, guardian.
July 1782.

I:155 LWT THOMAS HEWLETT 19 Mar 1787 Pr 10 Sept
1787.
To wife ANN HEWLETT, everything during her lifetime
at her decease to WILLIAM HEWLETT'S son THOMAS
HEWLETT and to MARTIN HEWLETT son of ALFORD HEWLETT
and to SUSANAH DARNAL'S son THOMAS DARNAL, to POLLY
LACY'S son STEPHEN LACY to be divided between them.
Exors: Wife Ann Hewlett, her father Samuel Moseley
and William Hewlett.
Wit: John Mitchell, Thomas Richardson, John (x)
Brown.
Sur for exors Ann Hewlett and Samuel Mosley are

George Hairston and John Salmon.

I:154 Inv & Appr HENRY PARR 21 Feb 1788 Retd 11
Mar 1788 by James Mankin, William Barton, Samuel
Clark..livestock, furniture..T:35.7.4

I:157 Inve & Appr JOHN RUSSELL 11 Mar 1788 by Hamon
Critz, John Parr, John Fletcher..T:7.0.9

I:157-158 LWT HENRY BARKSDALE, in good health...14
Feb 1778 Pr 12 May 1788.
Wife JUDITH BARKSDALE negros Thomas and James, and
all moveable estate during her lifetime, at her
decease to divided between: BEVERLY BARKSDALE, HENRY
HICKERSON BARKSDALE and UNITY MARTIN. To son DUDLEY
BARKSDALE 10 shillings; to son CLABAND BARKSDALE 10
shillings; to dau SARAH WATSON 10 shillings; to dau
MARY LINDSEY 10 shillings; to son JOHN BARKSDALE
10 shillings.
Appoint as executors John Barksdale and Brice
Martin.
Wit: John Dickerson, Sarah Barksdale.
Sec for John Barksdale, Robert Williams and John
Cox.

I:159 Inv & Appr HENRY MAYSE 12 May 1788 by George
Hairston, Alexander Joyce, Thomas Jamison..includes
horses, livestock, furniture T:79.13.4.

I:161 Inv & Appr DAVID REYNOLDS 26 Jan 1788 Retd 9
June 788 by John Cammeron, William Sharp, James
Taylor..1 negro, horse, gun, furniture T 61.6.0.

I:161-162 LWT JAMES TERRY 26 Jan 1788 Pr 9 June
1788
To my wife (not named) the land I purchased of Ralph
Shelton and personal estate not otherwise given. To
dau PEGGY negro Fillis; to dau SARAH who is married
to CUTHBERT SHELTON negro Gin; to dau PATTY negro
Sarah; to son JOHN land purchased from Abraham Eads
being 340 acres; to son RICHARD a horse.
Exors wife and Cuthbert Shelton.
Wit: Robert Hudspeth, William Williams, Robert
Hooker, Ralph Shelton.

I:162 Inv & Appr BAYNES CARTER 11 Aug 1788 by
Thomas Nunn, John Barksdale, John Pyrtle for a
T:2.17.9.

I:163 Acct of JOSEPH JONES by Admn Thomas Jones and
William Standefer
Pd Thomas Brandon, Peter Rickman, Henry Lyne and
Stephen Smith.
Cash of Moses Rentfro, Elijah Jones, George

Hairston. Retd 14 July 1788

I:164   Inv & Appr estate JOHN CUNNINGHAM 11 Aug
1788 by ..not named.. includes furniture, taylor
shears, cloth, tools T:17.12.10.

I:165 Inv & Appr estate HENRY BARKSDILL Retd 11 Aug
1788 by Thomas Nunn, John Redd, Alexander
Hunter..negro Tom, furniture, cow and calf, horse
T:52.2.6.

I:166 Acct of JOHN ROWLAND with Peter Saunders exor
12 Aug 1788.
Pd Thomas Prunty; Mrs Rowland for board of Garland
Akin, Henry Barksdill, Thomas Nunn, Sheriff for writ
on exors of Grimes Holcomb, Clerk of Henrico Co,
Col. Williams for attorney fees.

I:167 Inv & Appr estate THOMAS HEWLETT 17 Sept 1787
Retd 8 Sept 1788 by Henry Ines, Samuel Shoemake.
Thomas Richardson, one of the appraisers is now
deceased.
Negro Hannah, saddle, horse, furniture, livestock
T:109.6.0.

I:168-169 Acct of JOSEPH JONES
Payments to: John Rentfro, Thomas Brandon, Nicholas
Alley, Peter Saunders, Daniel Spangler, Swinfield
Hill, Henry Lyne, Thomas Prunty, Peter Rickman,
Brett Stovall, George Hancock, John Farguson,
William Standefer; Clerk of Franklin Co, Stephen
Smith.
Admn Thomas Jones.
Receipts: John Bates, Jeremiah Bohanon, John Fuston,
John Huff, William McCoy, Alexander Sutherland,
Elijah Jones, Ebenzer Pyott, Jesse Rentfro, Moses
Rentfro.

I:170 Inv & Appr estate ZACHERIAH MC GUIRE 25 Oct
1788 Retd 8 Dec 1788 by John Alexander, W. Pace,
Daniel Reamy
Furniture, cow, calf, yearling T:8.6.0.

I:171 LWT RALPH SHELTON SR 23 Apr 1787 Pr 30 Mar
1789
To my son JOHN SHELTON five pounds and no more. To
my last four children: EASOP SHELTON, ABBIGAIL
SHELTON, MARY SHELTON and LIBERTY SHELTON be raised
out of my estate. Remainder of the estate to be
equally divided between: RALPH SHELTON, PALATIAH
SHELTON, ELIPHAZ SHELTON, EZEKIAH SHELTON, JEREMIAH
SHELTON, AZARIAH SHELTON, ROGER SHELTON, EASOP
SHELTON, ABBIGAIL SHELTON, MARY SHELTON, LIBERTY
SHELTON, KATHERINE RUTHERFORD, SARAH ROBERTSON,
ELIZABETH ARNOLD, RINA MC GEHE, SUSANAH JONES.

23

Exors sons Ralph Shelton and Eliphaz Shelton.
Wit: John Fletcher, Henry Holt, John Branham.
Sec for exor Eliphaz Shelton are Stephen Lyon and
John Parr Jr.

I:172 Inv & Appr estate HENRY SHORT 20 Apr 1788
Retd 30 Mar 1789 by James Thompson, George Poor,
Abraham Frazier,..horse, tools, furniture T:13.5.0.

I:172 Acct of JOHN RUSSELL with William Barton admn.
30 Mar 1789
Payments to James Gibson, Jesse Adkins and Clerk.

I:173 LWT JAMES REA Sr, weak of body..11 Nov 1788
Pr 27 Apr 1789
Estate to remain with wife JOHNNA REA except the
smith tools to my son WILLIAM COLLINGS REA. After
the death of my wife the land where I live is to son
WILLIAM COLLINGS REA execpt the 40 acres where
Thomas Cooper now lives. I give to THOMAS COOPER
that 40 acres. To grandson JESSE ROCH ?furniture
and a horse. To my son JOHN REA, MARY ARS, REBEKAH
BOLLING, ANN BURNS and KATHERINE SANDERS one
shilling each. To my son JAMES REA one large bible.
The rest of my estate to be equally divided between
WILLIAM COLLINGS REA, ELIZABETH COOPER and SARAH
BOLLING.
Exors to be sons John Rea and William Collings Rea.
Wit: Robert Lorton, Thomas (x) Cooper, James Rea Jr,
William Collings Rea.
Exor W.C. Rea's sec: George Hairston and John Redd.

I:174 Inv & Appr estate RALPH SHELTON 30 May 1789
Retd 29 June 1789 by William Carter, George Carter.
Money scales, a still, furniture, livestock T:
51.10.6.

I:175 Inv & Appr estate ADAM LACKEY 29 June 1789 by
Francis Turner, Jeremiah Burnett, James Morrey?.
Livestock, horses, still, furniture and land
T:213.16.0

I:176 Inv & Appr estate JAMES REA SR 15 JULY 1789
RETD 27 JULY 1789 by John Wash, W. Pace, John Pace
Livestock, furniture, tools, geese, bee hives
T:49.14.3.

I:177-180 LWT MORDECIA HORD 29 Sept 1783 Retd 29
June 1789..
At this time about to start out to Powells Valley,
but being in perfect health, but danger of my
intended journey do make this LWT. My land lying on
the Western Waters to be divided in four equal parts
for my four sons STANWIX HORD, WILLIAM HORD, JOHN
HORD, MORDECIA HORD they are to draw lots. To son

24

MORDECIA HORD the land and plantation on Smith River where I now live, 6 negros: Else, Nann, Lett, Len, Anthony, Sirus, 250 pounds out of debts due me and one-third of all furniture, stock, crops and any other estate. My friend George Waller and my son William Hord to be his guardian and to educate him in the genteelest manner, send him to the Academy in Prince William County or another to be taught languages and sciences till 19 yrs of age then to be put to the study of Law or Physic to be his choice till age 21 yrs. To my dau MARY HORD negros: Agg, Winn, Randolph, Milly, Bess and 100 pounds and other personal property and to receive 1/5 part of all moveable property and everything remaing after Mordecia has his part.
To my son STANWIX HORD negros: George, Marge and Sall and personal property.
To son WILLIAM HORD negros Tom, Frank and Luce and personal property.
To son JOHN HORD negros Kate, Charles, Bett and Pegg and personal property.
To dau JANE FLEMING wife of John Fleming, negros Rachel, Mima, Peter and personal property.
Appoint as exors son William Hord, Patrick Henry, George Waller and Edmund Lyne.
Wit: Edmund Lyne, John Cox, Samuel Crutcher, John Barksdale.
Exors William Hord and George Waller have as sec: Henry Lyne, John Barksdale, Ignatious Simms.

I:180-181 LWT MANOAH CHAVIS, being sick and weak..19 Jan 1789 Pr 30 Nov 1789.
To PATTY EARL 100 ac of land and all my estate except 1 bed and cow I give to NANCY BIGERS EARL.
Estate to pass to Nancy Bigers Earl at Patty Earls death.
Exors John Nance, Jacob Warwick, Patty Earl.
Wit: Richard Mitchell, William Brown, John Haley.

I:181-182 Accts estate DAVID REYNOLDS 30 Nov 1789
Pd John Marr, A. Hughes, George Hairston, John Clark, Henry Lyne, Andrew Woolverton, John Staples, Isaac McDaniel, Moses Reynolds, Sheriff David Reynolds.
Receipts; David Reynolds his debt of Soloman Stevens, David Going (of Moses Hanks), Jacob Adams, Abraham Penn, John Gates.
Moses Reynolds, Admn.

I:182 Inv & Appr WILLIAM WOODS 9 Jan 1790 by Joseph Anthony, Robert Stockton, John Stokes.
One black walnut desk, surveyors chain, a red pocket book, small box T:6.5.0.

I:182-186 Inv & Appr estate MORDECAI HORD 6 Oct 1789 by John Salmon, John Redd, James Baker and John

Cox.
Negros: Lot, Ailse, Nance, Hannah, John, Cirus,
Phill, Charles, Bob, George, Jenny, Santy, Frank,
Ingram, Winney, Agee, Milley, Harry, Sall, Randolph,
Madge, Luce, Bett, Pegg, Peter, Anthony, Margery,
George, Kate, Phillis, Robbin, Bess, smith tools,
wagon, plantation tools, horses, large bible, 7 vols
Shakespeare, 7 vols of Pope, 2 parcels of books,
furniture, silver watch and livestock. T:1809.0.2.

I:186-187 LWT CHARLES BURNS SR 3 Apr 1789 Pr no
-sick and weak..to wife ANN BURNS the land where I
now live and estate for life. At the decease of
wife Ann the estate to be divided among my children
as follows: Son ALEXANDER BURNS one shilling; to
son SAMUEL BURNS one shilling; to son JOHN BURNS
one shilling; to son CHARLES BURNS JR one shilling.
The balance that remains to be divided between my
two sons ANDREW BURNS and WILLIAM BURNS and they
are to be executors.
Wit: John Pace, Robert Lorton, John (x) Ray.

I:187-188 Acct estate MORDECAI HORD 25 Mar 1790
Pd Jacob McCraw, Henry Sumpter, Richard Bradbury,
James Taylor, Joseph Cooper, John Cox, David
Anderson, George Waller, Mrs. Jarvis, John
Dillingham, John Salmon, Robert Williams, John Redd.
Payments to legatees: Thomas Jett, John Hord,
William Hord, Stanwix Hord and John Fleming.

I:189 LWT DAVID CLARK 20 May 1790
Weak in body..estate to be divided between my wife
ELIZABETH CLARK and my son GEORGE CLARK except that
my lands to my son George Clark when he comes to
lawful age. Appoint my father SAMUEL CLARK to raise
my son and educate him.
executors to be Samuel Clark Sr and Alexander Joyce
Sr.
Wit: John Nicholas, Samuel Clark.

I:189 Acct estate MARY LOGAN with Admn Hamon Critz
Sr 26 Oct 1790.
Pd for coffin, burial furniture, and for burying
said Mary Logan T. 5.0.0.

I:190 Division of estate WILLIAM STANDLEY 22 Oct
1790 by Larkin Turner, Daniel Smith, William Turner
and George Reives.
Ten children, each to receive 6.6.11 (not named)

I:190 Inv & Appr estate JESSE TATUM 24 Nov 1790 by
James Lyon, Jonathan Hanby, Stephen Lyon
Cattle, horses, furniture T:32.1.0

I:191 Acct estate JOHN GOODE 4 Dec 1790 by Exors
William Hunter and Thomas Cooper.

I:191-192 LWT WORHAM EASLEY 12 Aug 1790
-weak in body.. To son JOHN EASLEY five shillings;
to son MILLER EASLEY five shillings; to dau SUSANNAH
FRANCEY five shillings; to son DANIEL EASLEY five
shillings; To son JOSEPH EASLEY five shillings; to
son WORHAM EASLEY land whereon he now lives; to son
WILLIAM EASLEY the land where I now live being part
in Virginia and part in North Carolina and one
horse. To dau JUDAH EASLEY negro Lucy and a mare.
Lend to my wife NANNEY EASLEY all other estate for
life and at her decease to dispose of as she thinks
proper.
Appoint wife and son Miller Easley exors.
Wit: John Marr, Susannah Marr, Sarah (x) Walker.

I:192-193 Acct estate JOSEPH ANTHONY 28 Jan 1791
with Thomas Cooper and James Anthonys Exors.
1785-1786 Pd: Martha Dawson, Thomas Cooper, George
Hambleton, Abraham Penn, Joseph Cooper, Josiah Shaw,
George Hariston, William Graves, John Salmon,
expenses for going to Bedford Co.
Receipts: John King, Thomas Stovall, Edmond Winston,
Josiah Shaw, William Mills, John Rowland, George
Hairston.

I:194 LWT FRANCIS GILLEY 24 Dec 1790
-being very sick and weak..
To son RICHARD GILLEY 250 ac on Turkey Cock Crk; to
son FRANCIS GILLEY 250 acs on Turkey Cock Crk; to
son CHARLES GILLEY 160 ac at the head of little
Turkey Cock Crk; to my wife (not named) the land
where I now dwell and negros Tobe, Addam and Jacob
and moveable stock during her lifetime. At the
decease of my wife, the land to my son GEORGE GILLEY
and the stock and personal property; to my dau NANCY
negro Addam; to dau ELIZABETH negro Jacob. The
balance of the property sold and divided among my
four sons. If my mare has a colt, it is to go to
son GEORGE GILLEY.
Appoint my wife and son exors.
Wit: William St. Cox, Moses (x) Wilson, Phillip
Broshears.

I:195 LWT JOSEPH CLAYBROOK 7 Feb 1783
-weak in body..My estate is to be divided between
all my children both in quantity and quality. My
wife is to have possession during her lifetime or
widowhood.
Appoint wife Mary Claybrook, James Garland and Hugh
R. Morris as exors.
Wit: John Bailey, Charles Patrick, John (x)
Randolph.

I:196-198 Inv & Appr estate DAVID CLARK 29 Dec 1790
by John Parr, Hamon Critz, Peter France.
Clothing, furniture, horses, cattle, negros John,
Luce, Chloe, Isaac, Ned, Stepney, Celia. T:409.19.5

I:199 Sales estate ARCHS. REYNOLDS 4 Oct 1791.
To: Jesse Reynolds, George Hairston, Moses Reynolds,
Jacob Adams Jr, Archs. Reynolds, William Sharp,
Abraham Penn, Shadrack Barrett, Bartemus Reynolds,
John Holt, Francis Holt, Samuel Mannen, William
Mannen, Widow Smith. T:50.7.6

I:200 Inv & Appr estate JOSEPH CLAYBROOK 10 Mar
1791.   Furniture,   tools,   negros Sam and Pegg
T:95.10.0.

I:200-201 Sales estate JOSEPH CLAYBROOK
Sells   total estate..Lucy Claybrook purchased bed and
furniture. T:119.4.5.

I:201 Acct estate JOHN BLAGG with William Tunstall
Exor.
Pd: Daniel Haskins, John Aylette, John Salmon, Dr.
Rheyms,   Merry Webb, Thompson Dickinson, William
Swanson, Nicholas Darnold, William Craghill, John
Wells,   Larkin   Tarrent,   Lewis Gwilliam, Joseph
Bowling, William Clark, James Tarrent, John Cox,
Pittsylvania Co., George Elliott, Barnards, William
Fleming, Hugh Innes, Watts.

I:203 LWT WILLIAM GRAVES SR 12 May 1790
To my wife MARY GRAVES during her lifetime, the
tract of land where I now live and negros Martin,
James, Daniel and Martin's wife Betty, household
goods and stock except some horses.
To son THOMAS GRAVES negro Will when he is of age or
married and negro Daniel at his mothers decease and
the land where I now live.
To dau POLLEY GRAVES negros Black Betty and her
children Lucy and Diner and one horse.
To my dau SALLY GRAVES negros Rachel, Isaac and
Davy, 20 pounds and a horse when she comes of age or
marries.
To dau BETSEY GRAVES negros Mary, Samuel and Ford,
one horse and saddle when she comes of age.
To dau NANCY PARBURY negro Lucy and Peter.
To dau SUSANNAH MARTIN negros Ralph and Doll.
To son JOHN GRAVES at his mothers death negro
Martin.
To son WILLIAM GRAVES negro James at his mothers
death.
At the death of my wife that part of the estate lent
her and the balance of the estate to be equally
divided among all my children.
Appoint son Thomas Graves and Joseph Anthony exors

and my wife.
Wit: D. Lanier, Joseph Bouldin.

I:204-205 LWT SARAH HALL 23 Mar 1790 Pr 30 May 1791
-sick and weak..To my son NATHAN HALL all my negros:
George, Sarah, Rachel, Jane, Daniel, Sivey, Charles,
Price and Lijah my furniture and stock except two
cows. At my sons death the estate goes to my
grandchildren as Nathan Hall sees cause to divide.
My son is not to sell or dispose of any part of the
estate during his lifetime; should he do so, sell
and convey out of his hands and give to my grandsons
JOHN, RANDOLPH, THOMAS ROW and JONATHAN HALL any
part of the estate Nathan Hall might dispose of.
Appoints son Nathan Hall exor.
Wit: Jonathan Hall, Nancy (x) Storm, Elizabeth (x)
Storm.

I:205-206 Acct estate MORDECAI HORD 15 May 1791 with
exors William Hord and George Waller.
1789-May 1791
Pd: Jesse Maupin, James Baker, John Redd, Eusebus
Stone, Thomas Cunningham, Junor Meredith, William
Thompson, Stanwix Hord, John Hord, William Martin
for service in South Carolina, Tax 1786; William
Elkins waggoner, Sheriff of Franklin Co tax 1789,
Peter Rickman, Zack. Going, Joseph Phifer, to Henry
Lyne for Mathew Mullings, William Chandler, George
Penn, Samuel Crutcher, to Thomas Jett a legatee,
William Hord.
Receipts: James Baker, John Hord, William Hord,
Stanwix Hord, Thomas Jett, Peter Rickman, Henry
Lyne.

I:207 LWT THOMAS LOCKHEART 24 Nov 1790 Pr 30 May
1791
-sick and weak..to wife ELIZABETH LOCKHEART land and
plantation where I now live, negro Juda, stock and
furnishings during her lifetime.
To son THOMAS LOCKHEART 100 ac off the upper end of
the tract where I now live.
To son RICHARD LOCKHEART five pounds.
To son DAVID LOCKHEART tract of land formerly
divided from my land for Thomas.
To son ROBERT LOCKHEART negro Lue at his mothers
death.
To dau MARGARET TEDFORD two pounds at her mothers
death.
To dau AGNES SLAUSE two pounds at her mothers death.
To son WILLIAM LOCKHEART remainder of the land,
plantation and negro Tabby at his mothers death.
To dau MARTHA negro Judah.
Any remaining part of moveable estate that is left,
to be disposed of by my wife.
Appoint wife Elizabeth Lockheart and George Dodson

Sr as exors.
Wit: John Sharp, Robert Sharp, Margaret (x) Dodson.
Sec for exors: Samuel Crutcher, John Cammerson,
Richard Pilson.

I:209 Inv & Appr HENRY BUTLOR 23 July 1791 by Jacob
Farris, John Stokes, James Anthony..clothing, tools
T:10.5.0

I:209-210 Inv & Appr WILLIAM GRAVES 5 Aug 1791 by
George Hairston, Reuben Payne, John Alexander, Brice
Martin.. 8 horses, furniture, stock T:469.7.3.

I:211-212 Inv & Appr THOMAS LOCKHEART 30 July 1791
by John Pulliam, William Sharp, John
Randals..negros: Juday, Taby, Lurany, 4 horses,
stock, furniture, tools T:206.5.0

I:212-213 LWT JOHN MORGAN 22 Nov 1787
-sick and weak.. To my son WILLIAM MORGAN one
shilling.
To my dau ELIZABETH CLOUD a feather bed after my
wifes death.
To my dau KIZAH ELKINS a cow and calf, feather bed.
To my dau MARY HOPPER a cow and calf, a feather bed.
To my son JOHN MORGAN one shilling.
To my dau BASHABA MORGAN one shilling.
To my dau ANNA MORGAN one shilling.
To LITTLEBURY MORGAN one shilling.
To LUCY MORGAN one shilling.
To my wife MARY MORGAN stock, blacksmith tools,
furniture, guns during her lifetime and at her death
to be equally divided between my children:JOHN
MORGAN, BASHABA MORGAN, LITTLEBURY MORGAN, ANNA
MORGAN, LUCY MORGAN. If JOHN MORGAN leaves us, then
nothing.
Appoints my wife and son-in-law William Cloud as
exors.
Wit: William Winstead, Dutton Lane Sr, Dutton Lane.

I:213 Inv & Appr estate MORDECAI HORD 21 Mar 1791 by
Nathaniel Hix, Frederick Jones, David Lewis..cattle
T:32.8.

I:214 Acct estate JOSEPH ANTHONY 13 Oct 1791 with
Thomas Cooper and James Anthony exors.
Pd Clerk of Bedford Ct. yr 1773; Clerk of Henry Co;
Sheriff of Henry Co; Micajah Anthony for trip to
Albermarle Co, James Anthony.

I:215 LWT MARY ROWLAND
-perfect memory and sense..last will and testament
is recorded in the county court dated 17 Dec 1789.
I hereby revoke and disallow that part of the will

previously made as shall enslave negros Will and
his wife Betty. After my decease to be free and
emancipate them. They are to have one-fourth part
of my dead provisions on hand to support them, also
a cow and sow and the mare I have but if she has a
foal to my granddaughterLUCY RYAN..to have choice
iron working tools also.
Appoint George Rieves and William Turner attorneys
touching this matter.
wit: John Salmon, John Redd.

I:216 Inv & Appr JOHN RAMEY 24 Nov 1791 by John
Rowland, John Alexander, Brice Martin..negros
Siller, Joe, Mary, Jane, Jim, Dick, Milley ,Patty,
one horse, corn..T:316.10.

I:216-217 Inv & Appr MARY ROWLAND 3 Dec 1791 by
John Salmon, John Redd, George Waller.
Furniture, horses, tools, still, livestock negros
Will and Betty T:124.11.6.

I:217-219 Acct estate RALPH SHELTON with Eliphaz
Shelton exor.
Purchases for estate..cash from William Hooker. Pd
Clerk of Pittsylvania Co; John Redd, Col. Hughes,
Samuel Annett, M. Lawson, boarding widow and 5
children; corn for widow and 3 children for 1 year;
same for widow and 4 children 5 mos; 9 mos for board
of 2 children..pd Capt William Carter.
We have settled the account current of the estate of
Ralph Shelton. signed: James Lyon, Edward Tatum,
William Carter.

I:219 Inv & Appr WILLIAM DILLEN SR 21 Jan 1792 by
James Baker, Thomas Nunn, Michael Dillingham
Stock, gun, furnishings, tools, negros Dilce, Sue,
Tom. T:217.9.9.

I:219-221 Acct JOHN ROWLAND 30 Apr 1792 with Peter
Saunders.
1778-1792 payments to Clerk John Cox of Henry Co,
..Venable, John Staples, John Redd.

I:221-222 Acct JAMES HICKS Orphans by Alexander
Joyce.
1784-1787 Pd for cloth, shoes, board for three
children, tax. Pd George Hairston, board two
children one year (1786), D. Lanier, Gregory Durham,
School for two children, Board two children one
year. 1787 Benjamin Hix, Board two children one
year; deduct board of Polly Hix four years.
Wilks County, Georgia Alexander Joyce appeared in
Court and payments of account are just and true. 9
May 1790.

I:222 Acct estate JOHN BLAGGE 7 Mar 1792 with
William Tunstall, exor.
Tobacco to Walter Lamb for his brother Richard Lamb
in payment of a Bond 1778. Hire of four negros to
Thompson Dickerson.

I:223-224 LWT JAMES EDWARDS 9 Jan 1792
To my dau ELIZABETH EDWARDS five shillings.
To my dau RHODA EDWARDS five shillings
To my dau LAINEY COX five shillings
To my son LABAN EDWARDS five shillings
To my son JAMES EDWARDS five shillings
To my wife LUCY EDWARDS all the land that I possess,
390 ac m/l, house, furniture.
To my dau MARY EDWARDS at her marriage bed, cow and
calf, dishes.
To my dau JUDITH EDWARDS at her marriage bed, cow
and calf, dishes.
To my dau NANCY JOHNSON EDWARDS at the time of her
marriage bed, cow and calf and dishes.
To my wife Luce all the rest of my estate.
Appoints wife and Joseph Goodwin exors.
Wit:Dutton Lane Jr, Dutton Lane, William Hannah.
Codicil 13 Jan 1792..Wife Lucy Edwards to make a
title to the within metnioned land agreeable to a
Bond to John Marr. I give to my wife Lucy the
negros and corn for which I have John Marrs bond.
Wit; William Hannah, John Kelly, Joseph Goodwin.

I:224-225 Acct estate THOMAS LOCKHEART Sept 1792
Pd Col. Hughes, Col. G. Hairston, Henry Koger, John
Cox and cash of A. Penn.

I:225 Acct estate JOSEPH CLAYBROOK 8 Aug 1791 with
James Claybrook
1780-1788 Pd Sam. Shoats, Thomas Owens, Andrew Hart,
John Barsden, George Howl, William Watson, Thomas
Shiflot?, William Claybrook, James Oakes, John
Grogan, John ev..tt.
Receipts of James Lewis, William Langford, Edward
Burnett, Andrew Hart.
James Claybrook made oath before Joseph Scales that
seventy three pounds is due him of his father's
estate. 8 Aug 1791.

I:226-228 Inv & Appr estate THOMAS STOVALL by James
Taylor, William Moore, Daniel Taylor.
Plantation tools, furniture, negros Stepney, Toney,
Amey, Selah, livestock T:457.5.11.

I:228-229 Inv & Appr estate WILLIAM COX by Thomas
Chewning, William Mitchell, Jacob Kayton..furniture
and livestock T:36.15.

I:229-230 Inv & Appr estate JAMES EDWARDS by Dutton

Lane, John Kelley, William Rice..livestock, 2
negros, furniture, bond on Hampton Preston, Note of
Davis Mannen T:224.17.9.

I:230-231 Inv & Appr est DAVID CLARK 29 Dec 1790 by
Hamon Critz, John Parr, Peter France, Jacob
Critz..furniture, clothing, livestock, negros John,
Luce, Chloe, Isam, Ned, Stepney, Coley.

I-233-234 Division of that part of the estate now at
Capt. Clarks.
Clothing to negro fellow
Clothing given to orphans of John Frans.
John France's part of the estate which includes
negros Luce and children, Clory and Ned.
Division by A. Hughes, John Dillard, William Banks,
Hamon Critz.

I:234-235 DAVID CLARK'S estate with Samuel Clark Sr
guardian to George Clark orphan.
30 Nov 1790 - 20 Dec 1793
Supplies, paid taxes, pd Sheriff of Patrick Co, pd
Reuben Payne.

I:236-237 Acct estate HENRY PARR 12 June 1792 by
John Parr Jr Admn.
Nov 1788-June 1792 pd Dr Randleman, William Carter,
Hughes & Hairston, Benjamin Arnold, Palatiah
Shelton, James Shelton, John Parr Sr, Samuel Sharp,
William Fain.
Recipts; William Halbert, Peter Corn, John
Bottetourt, Zacheriah Keaton, John Parr Sr, William
Keaton, James Scurlock, Abraham Eades, Hamon Critz,
Humberston Lyon, Milly Parr, Stephen Lyon, George
Corn, Abraham Frazier, Arthur Parr, Nicolas Long,
James Baley.

I:237-238 LWT JAMES WILSON 27 Oct 1792
-sick and weak..To my wife during her natural life
or widowhood negros Nann, Betty, Ale and Sarah and
the rest of the estate until my two daus ELIZABETH
WILSON and SALLY WILSON arrive to lawfull age or
married, at which time to my dau ELIZABETH to have
negro Betty and my dau SALLY to have negro Ale.
POLLY HIX is to have my sorrel mare.
Appoint my wife, Thomas Vernon, William Shelton and
John Dillard exors.
Wit: George Fulcher, Judith Morris, Nancy (x)
Vernon, Nancy (x) Morris.

I:238-239 LWT JOHN PYRTLE 9 June 1793
Lend to my wife ESTER PYRTLE whole of my estate
except for the plantation working tools and
carpenter tools. At her death the estate to be
divided among all my children.

To my dau FRANCES CUNNINGHAM all the property lent

her when she married also my plantation tools and carpenter tools.
To my son JOHN PYRTLE five shillings after the death of his mother.
To dau MARY PYRTLE five shillings after death of mother.
After the death of my wife, the estate to be divided between my other four children when the come of age or marry being my dau MARGET SUMPTER, sons SAMUEL PYRTLE, JOSEPH PYRTLE and NANCY PYRTLE.
Appoint Harrison Hobard and John Philpott exors and guardian of my children.
Wit: Thomas Posey, John Smallman, Nathaniel (x) Rogers.

I:240 Inv & Appr estate JAMES WILSON 14 Sept 1793 by John Staples, Nathaniel Bassett, Joseph Morris, Samuel C. Morris.
Negros Nancy, Betty, Alley, Sarah, furniture, livestock T:270.3.9.

I:241 Inv & Appr estate JOHN PYRTLE by John Philpott, Eusabus Stone, William Turner..negro Nell, furniture, tools, livestock T:93.2.5.

I:242 Acct estate JOHN GOODE
Sales to; Soloman Jordon, Joseph King, Jeremiah King, William Heard, John Dillingham, John Burks, Thomas Cooper, Joshua Dillingham, Thomas Crag, Thomas Parsley, Patrick McBride.

I:243 Acct estate WILLIAM DILLEN 28 Mar 1794 with Benjamin Dillen exor.
Pd Henry Lyne, Robert Williams, Dr Cole, Thomas Hambleton.
Receipts: James Baker, Mayo Carrington

I:244-247 Inv & Appr est JOHN MARR
Furniture, guns, livestock, tools, negros:Ned, Ellet, Eady and 2 children, Aggey and 2 children, Cloway and 1 child, Sharper, Jack, Efram, William, Polley ,Francis T 1260.0.7. By William Mitchell William Hulet, John Pace.

I:247 Additions to the estate fo BENJAMIN COOK 8 June 1791 by Hugh Innis and William Ryan. negros Fanny and Silvia T:65.0.0.

I:248 Dower of MARY COOK widow of BENJAMIN COOK 18 May 1788 Retd 28 Apr 1794 with Benjamin Cook admn.
One-third part 163.9.4 and chooses negros Ben and Jude. By Hugh Innis and William Ryan.

I:248-249 Acct estate BENJAMIN COOK 20 June 1791.

Pd Nathaniel Abney, Abraham Abney, Francis Smith, Hawskins exors, recovering 3 negros in Ga.
Receipts Abraham Hendrick, Hugh Patrick.

I:249 LWT JOHN COX 2 Apr 1794
Wife LEANNER COX to have land, house, livestock and furniture until my son REUBIN COX is 21 yrs of age. Appoints Henry Grogan and my Brother Charles Cox as exors.
Wit: John Clifton, Thomas Cox.

I:250 Estate acct WILLIAM DILLEN with Benjamin Dillen 19 Feb 1795..pd Clerk John Cox, John Gossett.

I:250 Acct estate JOHN GOODE 30 Jan 1795..to settle account of Thomas Cooper against the estate.

I:251 Inv estate JOHN COX (no date) by Charles Cox, John Kelley, Joseph Goodwin..includes:cattle, one horse given to his son RUBIN COX, hoggs, gun and furniture...T:37.06.6.

I:252-253 Inv estate WALTER KING COLE Ret 27 Oct 1795
28 negros:Will, Bowser, Moses, Lewis, Joe, Sandy, John, Sarah, Phillis, Amy, Joe, Cela, Watt, Biddy, Peter, Kit, Tabb, Milly, Major, Rachel, Jacob, Polley, Lucy, Venus, Sall, Patts, Pegg, and Charlotte..horses, cattle, furniture, plantation tools..T:1251.7.7.
By John Rowland, J. Alexander, Sanford Ramey.

I:253-255 Inv JOHN WATSON 2 Nov 1795 by William French, James Cook, Thomas Vernon.
Family bible, books, Wesley's Sermons, 4 vol Fletcher's works, Haleys Life, testament, hymn book, children's instructions, dictionary, Lectures on the Trinity, spelling books, Latin, Nelson's Justice, Mariners Compass, Treatise on Medicine and Complete Surgery; furnishings, livestock T:130.12.7.

I:255-256 Acct DAVID CLARK with Samuel Clark, Sr. 8 Jan 1794
Pd for miscellaneous supplies, one years schooling, taxes
Rec'd for sales of various items.

I:256-257 Acct est JOHN WILLIAMS with William Brown and James Williams, exors.
1779 pd JOHN WILLIAMS a legatee, WILLIAM WILLIAMS, a legatee, THOMAS COOPER for the legacy of ELIZABETH WILLIAMS; REUBEN NANCE a legatee; JOHN MINTER for his own and SILAS WILLIAMS legacies.

I:257-258 Acct est RICHARD HOLT Ret 28 March 1796

with MILDRED HOLT Admn
Pd: Clerk of Henry Co, Sheriff, Dr. Cole, Daniel
Goldsby for William Graves; John Weaver, George
Hairston..pd food and clothing 5 small children 10
years, food and clothing for WILLIAM HOLT and
FIELDING HOLT sons and orphans 2 years, until their
own labor supported them.

I:258 Inv est JOHN HENRY 21 May 1796
Negros: Frank, Eave, Sam, Molly, Namon, Sally, 6
horses, cattle, furniture T:377.8. by David Lanier,
J. Alexander, Joseph Bouldin.

I:259-260 Acct est JACOB LINDSAY Retd 23 July 1796
by James Lyon, Admn
1790-1796
Pd John Marr's order for Edmond Winston; John Taylor
atty; John Marshall atty; Thomas Jamison, William
Easley, Hughes & Hairston, Eliphaz Shelton,
..Rentfro, James Lyon for attending Buckingham Co
court, Caleb Floid, John Tatum, Trent & Co, John
Cabell, Patterson & Smith, Dr Randleman.
Rec: sale of tobacco, negros Adam, Nancy, Ditcher,
Bob, George, Jane, Nelly, Rachel, Will, Ben & Elly
sold to satisfy debtors.

I:261 Acct est JACOB LINDSAY Retd 23 July 1796 with
James Lyon Sr.
1789-1794
Pd taxes on negros in North Carolina till 1794, same
in Virginia and two additional years. Sundry items
for Caroline Lindsay and Patsey Lindsay, schooling
for Jacob Lindsay for one year.

I:261-262 LWT WILLIAM STONE 7 Nov 1795
-weak in body..land and moveable property to wife
ELIZABETH STONE, son THOMAS STONE and the child she
is pregnant with also negro Tiller. Appoints wife
Elizabeth Stone and brothers Micajah Stone and
Eusebus Stone exors.
Wit; James Baker, Samuel Critchfield, Charles
Hibbert, William Ross.

I:262-263 LWT JOSEPH SCALES 13 June 1796
Son NICHOLAS SCALES to have land on the Holston
River known as the Daniel Tract being 400 acres.
Sons JOSEPH SCALES, HENRY SCALES and ROBERT SCALES
the tract on Dan River in Rockingham Co. N.C. 335 ac
and the remaining part of my land in the Western
Country in company with Nicholas Perkins and Hardin
Perkins to be equally divided. To son CONSTANT
SCALES 475 ac at the lower and east end of the
tract whereon I live and negro Aaron. To son PETER
PERKINS SCALES 600 ac, the remaining part of the
tract whereon I now live and negro Shadrack. To dau

POLLY JACKSON negros Synthia and Minn now in her possession, a horse, saddle, and bed and furniture. To dau BETHENIA SCALES negros Harry and Jenny, horse, saddle, two beds and furniture. To dau SUSANNAH SCALES negros Edmund and Siva. To dau ANNEY HARDEN SCALES negros Greenberry and Mintran. To dau BETSY SCALES negros Beth and Peggy.
The youngest children:Joseph, Henry, Constant, Peter, Susannah, Anney Harden and Betsy Scales should have a horse, saddle and beds and furniture when the marry or come of age.
Lend to wife ANNEY SCALES 8 negros during her natural life or widowhood to wit: Ned, Catoe, Ben, Peter, Stephen, Bill, Cloe and Phebe and the land where she now lives for life. At her death the negros lent her to go to the children as the rest of my estate not designated. Appoint wife Anney Scales, sons Nicholas, Joseph and Henry Scales and my brother Nathaniel Scales exors.
Wit; Henry Scales, Nathaniel Scales, Bethenia Scales.

I:264 LWT JOSEPH MORRIS 3 Mar 1796
-sick and in a low state of health..to wife MARY MORRIS all of the estate to enjoy during her natural lifetime and at her decease to all the children, namely: JUDITH MORRIS, JOSEPH R. MORRIS, LUCY MORRIS, GEORGE MORRIS, ARCHIBALD MORRIS, FAR... MORRIS.
Appoint John Dillard, Samuel C. Morris exors.
Wit: Thomas Dickenson, William French, Hezekiah Salmon.

I:264-266 Acct MORDECAI HORD Ret 28 Nov 1796
Pd Chadwell for taking care of the cattle in Powells Valley; John Redd, Samuel Crutcher, A. Hunter and wife; suits Hords exors vs Davis; Benajmin Dillen vs the Exors; Hords Exors vs Rickman; Hords Exors vs Brice Martin; E. Jarvis, Spencers Exors, William N. Venable, Jimmy James, William McRoberts, John Henderson, Francis Preston, Benjamin Dillen, Brice Martin, Clerk of Montgomery Co; Sheriff of Patrick, William Turner; William Hord for 3 journeys to S.C. gone 34 days; Thomas Jett going to Charleston 21 days and 17 days to Statesborough, S.C. Stanwix Hord a legatee, John Walton.
Recd of: William Elkins, Samuel Keeth, William Shelton, William Rowland, Christopher Bouldin, Peter Saunders.

I:266-269 Inv est JOSEPH SCALES (no date)
Negros:Ned, Cato, Ben, Stephen, Will, Peter, Harry, Edmond, Greenberry, Bethell, Amos, Shadrack, Phebe, Chloe, Jane, Silva, Mintaan, Peggy. 50 hd cattle, 78 hd hogs, 18 hd sheep, 12 horses, copper still,

plantation tools, 1000# tobacco, 3267#pork, 278 bu
corn, furniture..T:1590.0.10.
By: Dutton Layne, Thomas Chowning, William Hewlett

I:270-271 Inv est JOSEPH MORRIS 3 Feb 1797
Negros: John, Jupiter, Diah, Nerow, Cloe, Jane,
Dinah, 4 horses, cattle, tools, furniture T:799.10.4
by John Dillard, John Staples, Jesse Witt, Nathaniel
Bassett, Samuel C. Morris.

I:272-277 Acct est JOHN MARR by Susannah Marr
Pd: Miller Easley, John Pryors expense to New London
and Salem, John Clark, Elizabeth Perkins, M.
Perkins, est of James Edwards, Tax Pittsylvania Co,
Dr. Watson, John Dandrdige, Robert Hudspeth, Letter
of Admn in N.C., David Scales, Samuel Shelton,
William Mitchell, Nathaniel McGufford, Richard
Manley, Abraham Penn, Dudley Stevens, William
Stevens, William Cooksey, Charles Oakes, Isham
Laneford, George Davis, John Hampton, Reuben Payne,
William Hancock, John Lemmons, Peter Perkins, John
McRea, James Edwards, Thomas Jones, Lucy Caren,
Pareel Howel, John Redd, John Wilson, John Harris,
Thomas Perkins, Jonathan May, Jesse Atkinson, Jonas
M. Holland, Joseph Goodwin, Daniel Morrow, Samuel
Duvall, Robert Hughes, John Carter, Edward Cason,
Jere. Norris, Michael Swingle, Thomas Jones, Henry
Lansford, W. Horton, Nathaniel Durham, D. R. Dunlap,
Watson Gentry, Comfort Young, Foxhall Starman,
William Jones, Francis Cox, Frederick Black, William
Leonard, Thomas Mitchell, John Brown, William
Barker, John Rea Sr, John Dabney, Joshua May, James
May, Caleb May, Abraham Bostick, W. T. Morton.
Rec: Chandler Oakes, Rhodham Moore, George F.
Harris, Ware Stokes, Joseph Rice, William Nance,
William Hampton, George Britton, Thomas Stovall,
Joel Rice, William Mitchell, John Price, J.
Alexander, Reuben Payne.

I:277 Acct JOHN PYRTLE 13 May 1797 with John P.
Pyrtle.
Pd George Hairston, John Cox, William Sumpter, Henry
Lyne, William Turner, Joel Smith, John Philpott,
William Adams.

I:278 Acct WILLIAM DILLEN SR Ret 10 Feb 1796 with
Benjamin Dillen
Pd John Smith, Clerk of Henry Co, Augustine Lawless,
William Richardson.
Rec: a negro woman and child sold by the Sheriff.
Cash pd Susanah Dillen.

I:279-280 Acct JAMES SHELTON 25 Aug 1797 with
William Shelton, exor.
Pd William Shelton, George Hairston, Jesse Reynolds,

Samuel Kemp, Richard Welch, Samuel Staples, James Standefer, Drury Salmon, Haynes Morgan, Dr. Briscoe, D. Ross.
Rec: Cash lent me by my father James Shelton, Paige Oliver, Samuel Keaton, William Mills, William Shelton, John Redd for Alexander Joyce, sale of negro Kate to satisy David Ross execution.

I:280 Inv est THOMAS FARRIS 7 Oct 1797
Horse, furniture T:9.12.0

By: James Rea, John East, Joel Pace, Merry Webb.

I:281-282 Inv est WILLIAM STONE 13 Dec 1797 Ret 25 Dec 1797 by James Baker, John Philpott, S. Hord, Thomas Nunn.
negro Tiller, furniture, cattle, horses T:120.3.0

I:282-284 Acct est DAVID CLARK 4 Dec 1797 Ret 27 Jan 1798 with Samuel Clark Sr Admn.
Pd John Frans, Richard Hopkins, Aaron Mills, John Hall, Daniel Adams, supplies and schooling costs.
Rec cash from sundry sales.

I:285 Inv est RICHARD BRADBERRY 22 Feb 1798 Ret 26 Feb 1798
Tools, cow T:13.13.0.

I:286 Acct est THOMAS FARRIS Ret 27 Feb 1798 in acct with Judith Farris, Admn.
Pd taxes, John Hayns Rives, John Pace, William Pace Jr.

I:287 Acct est WILLIAM DILLEN SR Ret 26 Mar 1798 by Benjamin Dillen, Admn.
Pd Clerk of Henry Co, Nathaniel Shelton, John Dabney, John Solaman, Samuel Duvall, George Hairston.
Rec: sale to George Hairston, sale of shot gun..no T.

I:288 Division est WILLIAM DILLEN Ret 28 Mar 1798..Division among 7 legatees (not named) horses, negros, furniture.

I:289 LWT MARY REAMY 2 Dec 1797 Pr 28 May 1798
Weak in body..dau NANCY HAMBRICK negro Bell, bed and furniture, my wearing apparel, a mare, side saddle, chest and trunk..should any debts come against the estate or her securities Lewis Lee and Benjamin Jones the property be sold..but if not then goes as directed to Nancy Hamrick or her children. Appoint Benjamin Jones and Sanford Reamy exors.
Wit: Charles Philpott, Thomas Jones.

I:290-91 Inv est EUSEBUS STONE 22 June 1798

Negros: Isaac, Davy, Bet, Ross, Naka, horses,
cattle, furniture, tools T:548.1.0 by John Redd,
Joseph Anthony, Henry Clark.

I:292-294 LWT HENRY DILLEN SR 8 May 1797 Pr 26 Mar
1798
-weak in body...wife MARY DILLEN all the estate
during her natural life or widowhood..All daughters
PHEBE DILLEN, SUSANAH DILLEN, SARAH DILLEN may
remain at the plantation as long as they are single
and unmarried, but no longer.
To sons CARTER DILLEN, HENRY DILLEN, WILLIAM DILLEN
at the death of wife and marriage or death of my
three daughters to have 840 ac in Henry County, to
be equally divided among the afore named sons. Son
JOHN DILLEN after the decease of wife Mary, to have
negro Frank. To daus PHEBE DILLEN and SUSANNAH
DILLEN beds and furniture; to dau SARAH DILLEN now
married to JOSEPH CARTER three cows. After the
decease of my wife the negros: Jean, T.., Fann,
Betty, Tom, Jean and Phil to be sold if the legatees
can't agree to divide among my children to wit:
CARTER DILLEN, HENRY DILLEN, WILLIAM DILLEN, PATTY
DILLEN wife of WILLIAM DILLEN, PHEBE DILLEN, MARY
DILLEN wife of JAMES C. DILLEN, ANN COOK, SUSANAH
DILLEN and SARAH DILLEN. The balance divide between
daus PHEBE DILLEN, SUSANNAH DILLEN, SARAH DILLEN.
Wit: John Salmon, William Heath, Hezekiah Salmon
Codicil: If any of my sons or daus contends at law
for any part other than given them, their part is to
be divided among the others. 19 Oct 1797 Wit: John
Salmon, James Cook, Justiana (x) Heard.

I:295-296 Inv est WILLIAM KING 26 May 1798 Ret 25
June 1798
Cattle, horses, one negro, furniture, no T by
William Hewlett, John Davis, John Burgis.

I:296-298 Inv est HENRY DILLEN 10 Apr 1798 Ret 30
July 1798 by John Cox, Stanwix Hord, William Heath.
Horses, livestock, wagon, negro Fann, Jean, Cloe,
Phillip, Jean, Tom, Booker, Bell T: 794.15.5.

I:299 Inv est REUBEN VAUGHN 18 July 1798 Ret 25 July
1798 by Henry Clark, William Holt, Thomas Brown,
John Clifton..horses, furniture T 29.7.0

I:300 LWT PHILIP BRASHEAR Pr 30 July 1798
-very weak of body..to my wife ANN BRASHEAR all my
temporal estate, stock, household goods, land etc so
long as she lives and at her decease to all the
children then living. Appoint William Hewlett and
Joseph Goodman exors.
Wit: Arch. Murphy, George Gilley, Richard Gilley.

I:301 Inv est MARY REAMY 28 Aug 1798 by Jacob Farris, John Stokes, Charles Philpott
Negro, furniture, saddle T:107.3.5

I:302 Acct est RICHARD BRADBERRY Ret 24 Sept 1798 with Tabithia Bradberry, Admn.
Pd John Dabney, Samuel Duvall, taxes.

I:303 Acct est JOHN MARR Ret 24 Sept 798 with Susanah Marr Admn
Pd James Stewart, ..McRoberts, John. Wilson, Rice Hughes, John McRea, Robert Hannah, R. Payne for tax on a carriage, William French, R. H. Venable.

I:304-305 Inv est JOHN MASTERS 10 Dec 1798 Ret 28 Jan 1798
Livestock, plantation tools, furniture T:57.5.0.

I:306 Acct est WILLIAM WOOD Ret 24 June 1799 by Henry Lyne, Admn
Pd George Waller Jr, Henry McGuffy, Patrick Coleman, Robert Stockton, John Acuff, Moses Reynolds, Luis Davis, Blizard McGruder, John Cox, Richard Venable, Edward Henry, Thomas Stovall, George Hairston, Abraham Penn.
Rec: Alexander Hunter, Sales, Reuben Payne, Shadrick Going, William Hickenbottom, John Stuart, James Spencer, Ignatious Redman, William West, Walter N. Cole, Newsome Pace.

End of Will Book No. 1

II:1-2 LWT GEORGE KEY 1 Apr 1799 Pr 29 July 1799
To wife ISABELAH KEY 100 ac where I now live and negro Sary during her natural life, then to be divided among the children hereinafter named. The rest of the estate sold and divided among children: SUSANNAH MARTIN, TANDY CENTER alias KEY, DABNEY CENTER alias KEY, SALLY KEY, ONAH KEY, MARYANN KEY, GEORGE KEY, LUCINDY KEY, REBECKAH KEY. I give unto ALLEN CANNADAY five pounds.
All of my first children: THOMAS KEY, MILLEY TURNER, MARTHA STONE, CRASSEY KEY have received their part to keep and enjoy. If any of the first children not be satisfied with their part, may give in an account and come in as a equal part with the rest.

41

Appoint son Crassy Key, Tandy Center alias Key and
William Mitchell exors.
Wit: William Mitchell, Thomas Chowning.
Sur for William Mitchell is George Hairston.
Isabel Key one of the legatees, came into Court and
relinquished the legacy left to her by the Will and
claims a 1/3 part. dated 30 Sept 1799.

II:2-3 Acct est JOHN MARR Ret 30 July 1799
Pd Clerk of Henry Co; Clerk of New London, R.
Hannah, Sheriff Hairston, W. Mitchell, S. Standefer,
McCraw, Jesse Parks, S. Duvall, Clerk of Prince
Edward Co, Robert Maitland, Clerk of Buckingham Co,
M. Woodson.
Signed: Joseph Anthony, William Mitchell, John Pace.

II:4-5 Inv est BENJAMIN REA Ret 26 Aug 1799
Horse, livestock, tools, furniture T 68.11.6 by John
Wash, Benjamin Harrison Jr, Sanford Reamy.

II:6 Inv est JOHN HAMPTON 26 Oct 1799 Ret 28 Oct
1799 by Joseph Goodwin, Rees Hughes, James
Oakes..furniture T: 16.2.0.

II:7 Acct JOHN MARR 31 Oct 1799
Pd. George Hairston, Abezah Hughes, John Dabney,
Samuel Duvall, Clerk Of Henry Co., Clerk of
Pittsylvania Co.
Recd: Patrick Poutaince, Charles & Ferrell.

II:8-10 Inv est DAVID WEATHERFORD Ret 30 Dec 1799
Livestock, horses, furniture T:107.13.0 by Charles
Royster, Joseph Hopper, John Pace.

II:11-14 Inv est GEORGE KEY Ret 27 Jan 1800
Negros: Sary, Milly, Amy and children, Anney,
Hannah, Agnes, Robert, Manson, Pheby, livestock,
furniture, tools, smith tools, corn, fodder, cotton
T 107.12.6 by Rees Hughes, William Hewlett, Thomas
Chowning, William Mitchell.

II:14-15 Acct est JOHN GOODE with William Hunter
exor Ret 24 Feb 1800
Pd: taxes, William Tunstall, Capt. John Soloman,
Thomas Cooper, John Henderson, James Anthony, George
Hairston..
Rec: Thomas Cooper.

II:16 Division est JAMES SPENCER 4 Oct 1798 Ret 25
Feb 1800
An agreement between John Spencer, William Spencer
and John Dillard. To John Spencer the upper lot
over the creek, little Luce, Fanny, Joe. William
Spencer the lower lot negros Anaker, Gabriel, Sally.
George Washington Spencer house land, negros Easter,

Dolly, Nancy. James Spencer the Marrowbone land negros Dick, Ned, Amey.
By William Hill, William Shelton, Nathaniel Bassett, Samuel Jennings.

II: 17-18 Acct of DAVID CLARK with Samuel Clark Admn. 31 Mar 1800
Pd: taxes, personal items for George Clark, supplies, to Philpott for making a coat, to Reynolds for one years schooling.

II:19 Acct JOHN MARR to Thomas Hardman Ret 30 April 1800
Pd Clerk of Henry and Clerk of New London.

II:20-21 Dower of ISABELL KEY Ret 29 July 1800
One-third part of the estate of George Key, for the benefit of Isabell Key, widow and relict of said George Key to wit: negros Manson, Pheby, furniture, cattle 113 ac on Fall and Middle Creek, T 192.2.6. Signed: John Pace, P.H. Fontaine, John Alexander.

II:21 Acct sales of the estate of JOHN HAMPTON with Tabithia Hampton
To Daniel Wilson..no T.

II:22-23 Acct est JOHN WILLIAMS with William Brown and James Williams Ret 23 Feb 1801
Pd: Silas Williams, John Minter, William Hord, William Brown, Ruffen Brown, John Forsie, William Hunter, John Lovell, Robert Stockton, John Conway.

II: 23 Inv est WALTER KING COLE 11 Mar 1801 Ret 30 Mar 1801
Negros: Bowzer, Mousby, Lewis, Joe, Sandy, Amie and 4 children named Joe, Cole, Watt and Linda; Tabb and 5 children Milly, Margaret, Docea, Patty and Cretia; Rachel and 3 children Jacob, Andrew and Jinny; Polly and 4 children Lucy, Dolly, Becky and Silva; Venus and 2 children Armstead and Nelly; Charlotte, Sall, Kitty, horses, livestock, plantation tools, furniture T 1171.14.8.

II:25 Division est of WALTER K. COLE Ret 11 Mar 1801
To Benjamin (W.B) Harrison and Sally his wife..negros Bower, Joe, Rachel, Andrew, Jenny, Charlotte, Ame, Cele, Watt, Linda, Sl--, Jenny, livestock and furniture T 396.15.0 signed: P. H. Fontaine, William Mitchell, P. Garland.

II:26 Dower for Widow of WALTER KING COLE Ret 30 Mar 1801
One-third part of the estate of Walter King Cole for William Harrison, 290 ac for Sally Harrison, widow

43

of said Walter K. Co⌐e on Little Marrowbone Crk.
Signed: Thomas Barton

II: 27-28 Report of the division of the est of
WALTER KING COLE
To SAMUEL COLE negros Moses, Lewis, Joe, Tabb,
Milly, Mary, Docia, Patty, Cretea, Venus, Jacob,
Armstead, Nelly, Polley, Lucey, Dolly, Becky, Silva,
Sal, Kitty, Sandy, horses, livestock and furniture
T 774.19.8
By P.H. Fontaine, William Mitchell, P. Garland.

II:28-30 Acct est WALTER K. COLE with Benjamin
Harrison Ret 30 Mar 1801
Vouchers T 567.16.6
Rec: sale of seven negros, tobacco sales, corn,
wheat and rent of land to Sanford Reamy, Thomas
Leak, books sold to Dr. C. Cox.

II:30-32 Acct est WALTER K. COLE with Sally Harrison
Ret 30 Mar 1801
Pd services of Richard Curd
Rec: sale of crops

II:32-34 Acct est WILLIAM GRAVES with Joseph
Anthony exor. 30 Aug 1799 Ret 27 Apr 1801
Pd: George Hairston, Henry Clark, Miss Graves, T.
Graves, Green Bouldin, G. Taylor.
Rec: Thomas Bowling, James Rea, Nelson Phillips,
Mrs. Porter, Thomas Alexander, Thomas East, Luke
Adams, Joseph Anthony, B. Martin, Martin &
Gearheart.

II:34-35 Acct est WILLIAM GRAVES with Joseph
Anthony Ret 27 Apr 1801
Pd: J. Salmon, Joseph Martin, John Alexander, J.
Weaver, John King, W. Parberry, B. Rowland, Mary
Graves, Peter Garland, George Hairston, Henry Clark,
James Laremore, Thomas Brown, James Parberry and a
legatee Susannah Dillen.

II:35-36 Acct Div est WILLIAM GRAVES Ret 27 Apr
1801
Division of the residue of the estate to the
following legatees; JOSEPH MARTIN, WILLIAM GRAVES,
THOMAS GRAVES, THOMAS EAST, ROBERT ANDERSON, GREEN
BOULDIN, JAMES PARBERRY, JOHN GRAVES.
By George Hairston, Reuben Payne, John Alexander.

II:37-38 LWT JOHN GOING 27 Mar 1801 Pr 25 May 1801
-sick and weak.. dau NANCY GOING horse, cow and
calf, bed and furniture; to dau SUSANNAH GOING same,
to son SIMEON GOING cow, calf and furniture; to son
ZEDEKIAH GOING cow, calf and furniture; to son
JOSIAH GOING cow, calf, furniture; to son ZACKERIAH

GOING cow, calf and furniture; to son LITTLEBERRY GOING cow, calf, furniture; to son CLABOURN GOING cow, calf and furniture. Lend to wife ELIZABETH GOING during her natural life stock, household furniture, land, the plantation where I now live..at her decease the land in Henry and Patrick county to be sold and divided among all the children viz:Zachariah Going, Nancy Going, Susannah Going, Zedikiah Going, Simeon Going, John Going, Josiah Going, Zedekiah Going, Clabourne Going, Littleberry Going, Elizabeth Minor wife of Huckeah Minor.
Appt friends John Stone and John Cox Jr as exors.
Wit: John Cox, Usebeous Stone, Mary (x) Stone
27 July 1801 Elizabeth Going Admn with John Cox and Henry Clark sur.

II:39-40 Inv est JOHN GOING 11 Aug 1801 Ret 31 Aug 1801
Livestock, blacksmith tools, plantation tools, furniture, copper still T 325.7.3 by John Hord, Bartlett Wade, Stanwix Hord, John Cox Jr.

II:40 LWT WILLIAM THOMASON (no date) Pr 27 Oct 1801
To wife (not named) negros Sunder and Charlotte, household furnishings, stock, grain during her natural life. To son ROBERT THOMASON a horse or the value of one out of the estate when he comes of age. At the decease of my wife Estate divided equally among children: JANY, FLEMON, SARAH, PHEBE, ANNA, JOSEPH, JAMES, LYUS(Elias), WINNEY, AMALI, ROBERT and their heirs.
Appoint sons Fleming and Joseph Thomason exors.
Wit: John Wells, John Davis, Joseph Gravely
28 Sept 1801 Fleming and Joseph Thomason exors with John Marsten and John Conway their sur.

II:41 HENRY DILLEN, report of the property lines in the division of the land..mentions lines of William Dillen, Line between Henry Dillen and Carter Dillen. Signed: George Waller.

II:41-42 INV JOHN OLDHAM 23 OCT 1801 Retd Oct Ct 1801
Negros:Ben and Mary, horses, livestock, furniture, tools no T. By John Creasey, Henry Jones, John Gibson.

II:43 Nuncupative Will DUTTON LAYNE 4 Oct 1801 Pr 30 Nov 1801
-sick and weak...All that I have given to my sons SAMUEL LAYNE and DUTTON LAYNE and to dau ELIZABETH NORMAN I confirm. To dau SARAH LAYNE negro Hannah, bed and furniture. To the living children of my dau RHODY BEEN one hundred pounds in property and a

claim of debt of twenty three pounds which I have
against the estate of Robert Been to be equally
divided among them. The remainder of the estate to
my wife ELIZABETH LAYNE during her natural life then
to be equally divided among the children.
Wit: John Beck, Ann Beck
Elizabeth Layne apptd Exor with William Mitchell and
George Hairston sec.

II:44 Inv est JOHN THURSTON 20 Nov 1801
Furniture, tools, livestock T79.2.0 by Ruben Payne,
John Wash, Robert Anderson.

II:45-46 Inv est DUTTON LAYNE 25 Jan 1802
livestock, negros:Easter, Chester, Betty, Peter,
Lanns, tobacco, furniture, tools T:489.9.3 by
William Hewlett, William Mitchell, John Kelly.

II:47-48 Inv est JOHN BARKSDALE 11 Sept 1801 Ret 25
Jan 1802
Negros: Pen, Ned, Nelly, Sealy, Bob, Terry, Swenday,
Jim, Sucky, Lewis, Tiller, Jude, Anna, Gran, Milly,
Adam, livestock, horses, wagon, furniture T1280.3.9
by John Redd, Thomas Nunn, John Cox.

II:49 Acct est JOHN THURSTON 22 Feb 1802
Find the Acct on hand to be T 95.14.1 ..signed
Joseph Hobson, John Alexander, John Wash.

II:49-50 LWT SAMUEL LAYNE 17 Aug 1799 Pr 22 Feb 1802
My wife MOLLY LAYNE to have the land whereon I now
live during her natural life or widowhood, the use
of the personal estate until the last child is 21
yrs of age or marries subject to the maintenance and
education of all children. The personal estate to
divided my wife and children JEFF LAYNE, JOHN LAYNE,
RHODA LAYNE, NANCY LAYNE and SAMUEL LAYNE. The land
is to be divided between the children.
Wit: John Verell, Peter Sarreson, Dutton Layne.
II:50 codicil to the will of SAMUEL LAYNE 12 Feb
1802 Pr 22 Feb 1802
-weak in body..the dowry left me by my father DUTTON
LAYNE, I do give to my dear wife and children:
JEFFERY LAYNE, JOHN LAYNE, RHODY LAYNE, NANCY LAYNE
and SAMUEL LAYNE. If my wife has another child,
then to be treated equally with the other children.
The money due me in Franklin County to be also
equally divided.
Mary Layne, widow, and William Norman Admn with
Daniel Worham and Permenas Williams, sec.

II:51 LWT THOMAS CHEWNING 6 Sept 1801 Pr 23 Feb
1802
To wife HANNAH all the estate real and personal
during her natural life or widowhood. At her

decease or marriage the estate to be sold and divided among the children: ELIZABETH CHEWNING, ANNA CHEWNING, THOMAS CHEWNING, SARAH CHEWNING, CHATTEN CHEWNING, MILDRED CHEWNING, JOANNA CHEWNING, CATHERINE CHEWNING, WILLIAM COLEMAN CHEWNING, AILEY SALE CHEWNING.
Wife HANNAH CHEWNING to give at her discretion or as the children marry such things as she can spare and their value to be cut off their share.
Appoint sons THOMAS CHEWNING, CHATTEN CHEWNING and William Mitchell exors.
Wit: Philip Conner, William Hewlett, John Hamusende??.
Exors Thomas and Chatten Chewning have for sec. Joseph Martin and John Alexander.

II:52-53 Inv est SAMUEL LAYNE Ret 29 Mar 1802
Horse, livestock, furniture, no T by William Mitchell, Mason Kelly, William Hewlett.

II:53-54 Inv est THOMAS CHEWNING Ret 26 Apr 1802
Negros: Isaac, Agga, Jack and 2 others; 4 horses, livestock, furniture no T. By William Mitchell, John Kelly, Mason Kelly.

II:55-56 LWT THOMAS GARNER 27 Mar 1801 Pr 28 June 1802
-sick and weak..To my wife SARAH GARNER during her natural life or widowhood, the land and plantation whereon I now live. The stock and moveable property to wife Sarah to dispose of at her will and pleasure. The land, at her decease, to be equally divided between my two young sons WILLIAM GARNER and ABEL GARNER. To my dau DIANER CAHILL six shillings. To my dau NANCY HERD six shillings; to my son OBEDIAH GARNER six shillings, to my dau ELIN GARNER a bay mare, the first colt to my son JOHN GARNER, also to dau ELIN GARNER a bed, furniture, cow and calf. To son THOMAS GARNER a bay colt. At the decease of my wife, the stock and moveable estate to my four young sons:THOMAS, JOHN, WILLIAM and ABEL GARNER.
Appoints wife Sarah Garner and Jesse Heard exors.
Wit: William Heard, William Draper, Jane (x) Warrin.
Sur for exors are William Heard and John Cahill.

II:56-57 LWT JOHN STOKES 18 May 1802 Pr 28 June 1802
-sick and weak...to my dau POLLY STOKES a mare, colt, side saddle, 3 yr old filly, 2 feather beds and furniture, 2 cows and calves negro Jeney and all the corn and meal that is on hand at my decease, walnut chest, weaving loom and all flax and hemp on hand, 5 hd hogs, pr flat irons, plow chains, lg jar, black walnut table. To son WILLIAM STOKES saddle and 5 hogs. All other personal estate left to be

47

sold and proceeds to my two grandchildren; ELIZABETH
LUMPKIN STOKES and THOMAS HAILE STOKES and all
money due my estate divided among the above named
grand children.
Appt as exor Benjamin Jones.
Wit: Benjamin Jones, Reuben Nance, Nancy (x)
Langford.
George Hairston sec for exor.

II:57 Acct of WALTER K. COLE Ret 30 Aug 1802
In acct with John Alexander and Sanford Reamy
guardins for SAMUEL M. COLE orphan.
Pd: Luke Adams, Robert Alexander, George Hairston,
M. Randolph, Martha Fontaine, Peter Garland, Joseph
Hopson for board and schooling Samuel Cole;
Nathaniel W. Dandridge, Hugh Nisler for schooling;
Frederick Eckols, Thomas Jett for schooling; Robert
G. Payne, John Rowland, John East, Peter Gearheart,
Thomas Dix, William Moore.
Rec: Milly Milles, John Pace, William Dillen, Robert
Alexander, Brice Martine, Terry Hughes, Reuben
Payne, William Moore, Thomas Graves, John Wash, John
Alexander, Sanford Reamy, Robert Anderson, Thomas
East, Samuel Carr, Thomas Jett, John Rowland. No
total.

II:60 LWT JOHN WELLS 13 Mar 1802 Pr: 27 Oct 1802
-sick in body.. To wife JUDITH WELLS all my estate
both real and personal during her natural life,at
her decease to be equally divided between my six
sons and daus. Appoint sons MATHEW WELLS and
BARNABY WELLS as exors.
Wit: Edward Keernler??, Thomas Dickerson.
Exor Barna Wells with George Hairston sec.

II:61-62 Inv Est JOHN WELLS Ret: 2 Mar 1803
Negros: Feby, Mary, livestock, furniture, tools T
206.3.9 by Henry Karrunire, Benjamin Lanier, William
Larrimore.

II:62-64 Inv est JOHN STOKES Ret: 31 Jan 1804
Stock, horses, one negro, furniture T95.8.8 by Jacob
Farris, Charles T. Philpott, James Howard.

II:64-66 Inv est THOMAS GARNER Ret: 30 May 1803
Furniture, stock, tools, horses, no Total by William
Draper, Junor Meredith, John Parsley.

II:67-68 Inv est JOHN EAST Ret: 28 Mar 1803
Negros: Grace, Agga, Tab, Lucy, stock, horses,
furniture no T by Robert Anderson, John Wash,
William Dillen.

II:68-69 Inv est PHILIP BRASHEARS 30 May 1803
Furniture, no total, by William Mitchell, Davis

Burgess, John Burgess.

II:69-71 Inv est JAMES HUNT 20 May 1803
Negros: Aggy, Ruben, Harry, Sam, Ally, furniture,
livestock, no T by James Johnston, Thomas Dickerson,
Henry Lawrence.

II:72 Acct JOHN OLDHAM Ret 29 Nov 1802
Pd: John Dabney, William Carrington, B. Smith, John
Cox, George Hairston, Samuel Elliott, Robert
Stockton, John Gibson, Henry Clark, Peter Gearheart.

II:72-73 Acct JOHN THURSTON Ret 31 Aug 1802
Pd: Dillen's bond, B. Rowland Jr, N.W. Dandridge,
William Reamye, Thomas Dix, William Pace Sr, Luke
Adams, John Rowland Jr, Cocke & Co, Thomas Leak,
William F. Thurston, Thomas East T:94.5.9.

II:73-75 Inv est JOHN HORD Ret 30 Jan 1804
Livestock, horses, negro Cate and children Ales and
Surdy, Pegg, Ben, Bett, Nancy, Phillis, Becky,
Jeany, Rachel, Lett, George, John, Robin,
furniture..a horse sold Abel Willis before the
inventory..No total by John Redd, John Cox, Stanwix
Hord.

II:75-76 Acct GEORGE KEY Ret 28 Nov 1803 by William
Mitchell exor.
Pd: N.W. Dandridge, John Waller, divide among 15
legatees each 2.17.6 to 6 young legatees 43.11.
each..balance in favor of legatees 290.1.10.

II:76-78 LWT DANIEL REAMY Pr 29 Apr 1805
"I having a journey to go and heaving not a leace of
my life in case of death wold wish my Will be known
and understood"..to my wife MARY REAMY I leave the
plantation whereon I now live, negros Mary and Jim,
stock of all kinds and tools during her natural life
or widowhood, at her decease the land to be sold,
money divided between my three sons WILLIAM WHALEY
REAMY, JOHN REAMY, DANIEL REAMY. After my wife's
decease negro Jim to go to son JOHN. Negro Mary to
go to my dau RAMOTH REAMY also three children of the
said wench, Joseph, Fortin and Judy, if she should
die without issue then divided among all the
children. To son WILLIAM WHALEY REAMY negro Isack
and should he die without issue to all the children.
To dau JEMIMA HUGHES, negros Siller and Pat. To dau
LETTY HUGHES negros Grace and Aggy. To dau MARY
ALEXANDER negros Jinney and her children and at her
decease to two of her children: Boneparte Alexander
and Daniel Reamy Alexander. To dau NANCY ROWLAND
negro Sealy and her increase during her life then to
her children. "There is one point I wold observe
the negro wench Silver is not to be used ill in no
respect she is to live as a free woman and under the

49

care of my sons John Reamy and William Whaley Reamy
and they are to have power to remove her slavery and
make such satisfaction to Mr. Terry Hughes or his
wife as they think fit". The 370 ac tract on the
Richmond and Lynchburg Rd to be sold and the money
used for schooling my young son Daniel, to him 4
negros:Dick, Jacob, Chany and Fanny. Negro Milly to
continue with my wife during her life for the use of
maintaining a pore unhappy child of mine, the name
of BETSY REAMY, wife to dispose of said negro as
she thinks fit.
Wit: William Pace, John Creasy.
N.B. The negro Joseph I leave to Sanford Reamy and
his heirs with him giving me and my heirs an
indemnifying bond against the legatees of John Reamy
deceased. signed: Daniel Reamy
same witness.
Mary Reamey exor with John Reamy and William Reamy
her sec.

II:79 Acct GEORGE KEY RET 28 MAY 1804 in acct with
William Mitchell, exor.
1779-1802
Pd: Joseph Turner, J. Alexander, Robert Alexander,
John Burgess, Harrison Boyd, Crassey Key, William
Hewlett, William Cobler, Richard Stone, Isabel Key,
John C. Cox, Tandy Key.
Rec: Robert Stockton, Isabell Key, Crassey Key,
Josiah Turner, Elisha Gunn, Luke Adams, Randolph
Adams, Francis Gilley, George Gilley, Daniel Worham,
William Cobler, Samuel Layne, John Bailey, Dudley
Stephens, Reese Hughes, Samuel Elliott, Moses Smith,
William Turner, John Quarles, William C. Rea, Robert
Smith, Thomas Smith.

II:80 Div est WILLIAM ALLEN 3 Feb 1804 Ret 30 Apr
1804
By John Dillard, John Staples, Peter Garland
agreeable to the last will and testament of William
Allen. Property:negros Jacob, Sussey, Michael,
Jordon, Sally and 2 boys, Vine and children, Winney
and children..we divide as follows: To ROBERT ALLEN
negro Jacob and his paying estate 5.14.4.
To WILLIAM MILLS, negro Michael and pay 5.14.4 to
estate.
To JOSEPH ALLEN negro woman and child and to
receive from the estate 4.5.8. The residue of the
estate to be as per the Will.

II:81-82 LWT JOHN HORD 26 Aug 1803 Pr 28 Nov 1803
To wife RUTH HORD one half of the whole estate the
residue to my dau SALLY C. HORD. If my wife should
have another child then the estate to be divided in
three parts.

Appt Alexander Hunter, James Greenlee and Ruth Hord exors.
Wit: Washington Rowland, Peyton Hunter.
Exor Ruth Hord has as sec. George Hairston and Henry Lyne.

II:82-83 Dower Allotment to MARTHA HUNTER widow of ALEXANDER HUNTER Ret 26 Mar 1804
Negros Davy, Tiller, Sam, horse, furniture, livestock, tools..T (2 listed 484.17 and 485.16.9.)
By John Cox, Stanwix Hord, John Philpott, Samuel Philpott.

II-83-85 LWT ALEXANDER HUNTER 3 Nov 1803 Pr 27 Feb 1804
-being sick of body...to my wife MARTHA HUNTER one-third of the land, negros and moveable property and Hanners child named Cloe exclusion of her third to wait upon her during her lifetime and at her decease Cloe, Hanner's child left equally to PETER HUNTER, SAMUEL HUNTER, PEYTON HUNTER, ALEXANDER HUNTER and POWHATAN HUNTER. Wife Martha Hunter to have a third of all my other negros and moveable property and to have full power to leave her third of moveable property to any of the sons or daus as treat her best. The balance of the estate to be sold and when the sons come to age 16yrs they may take care of their own part which I have left them. The youngest childrens legacies to be left in the hands of the executors till they are 14 yrs of age then they may choose guardians for themselves. To dau PATTY SPENCER a negro and child, horse, furniture. To dau PERMELIA HUNTER negro Hanner and children Kiky and Sall, furniture, horse, cow and calf. To son ROBERT HUNTER $8.00. To dau RUTH HORD 5 shillings. To dau ELIZABETH MATHEWS $8.00. To dau POLLY BASSETT $8.00.
Appt as exors wife Martha Hunter, Peter Hunter, Samuel Hunter, Peyton Hunter and Alexander Hunter.
Wit: Elijah (x) Huhey?, Nancy (x) Huhey?, Young Burchett, John M. Boles.
Exors Martha Hunter and Samuel Hunter and Peyton Hunter have as sec. George Hariston, David Lanier.

II:85-87 Inv est ALEXANDER HUNTER 13 Mar 1804 Ret 26 Mar 1804
Furniture, plantation tools, horses, livestock, negros: Jim, Tiller, Abraham, Sally, George, David, Dick, Samuel, Cloe, Hessey, Hannah, Jack , sucky, Wagon, blacksmith tools, carpenter tools...no T.
By John Cox, Stanwix Hord, John Philpott, Samuel Philpott.

II:88-90 Sales est DAVID WEATHERFORD 2 Nov 1799 Ret 28 May 1804

To: George Gilley, James Brashears, Elie Bryant,
Wiatt Shelton, Daniel Reamy, John Carnal, Thomas
Hopper, Thomas Blakely, John Smith, John Rowland,
Terry Hughes, George Hairston, William C. Rea, John
Wilson Sr, John Wilson, John Burnett, Aaron Wilson,
Buckner Jones, Harden Weatherford, Nathaniel Durram,
Thomas Wilson, Judia Weatherford, Isbel Key, Wilson
Rea, Barna Burnett, John Hewlett, James Rea, Robert
Smith, Thomas Stewart, Luke Adams, Moses Wilson..no
total.

II:91-92 Acct DAVID WEATHERFORD Ret 28 May 1804
Rec: George Gilley, Eli Bryant, John Smith, Terry
Hughes, Judea Weatherford, John Rowland, George
Hairston, James Rea.
Pd:Thomas Dix & Co for Mary Weatherford, Joseph
Weatherford, Judith Weatherford, Benjamin
Weatherford, John Alexander, William C. Rea, Thomas
Wilson, Shelton & Pannel, Hardin Weatherford, Eli
Bryant, George Gilley.

II:92-93 Acct ROBERT HILL Ret 26 Mar 1804 in acct
with Thomas Hill.
Pd: James McKeacky?, Jesse Herd for John Wilkerson,
Robert Jones,
 Robert Wooding, Peter Saunders, John Dickerson,
William Ryan, Joseph King, William Terry for Richard
Turner's estate, James Beuser??, Thomas Hill a
legatee, John Murphy, John Dickerson and Edward
Choat.
Rec: William Manafee Sr, Shadrack Green, Callaway &
Early, James Callaway, James Dillion,

II:94-95 Inv est MARTHA WALLER Ret 16 July 1813
Negros: Pol, Martin, Matilda, Sarah, Richardson,
Eliza, Henrietta, Zilpah, 4 horses, oxen, wagon,
cart, furniture, books, livestock T2676.9.5. by P.H.
Fontaine, Thomas Starling, James Bouldin Jr..add 3
negros, still, 3 vols Dodrigers Works.

II:96 LWT JACOB FARRIS 11 Jan 1812 Ret Sept Ct 1813
To my wife my estate real and personal. To son
JOSIAH FARRIS negro Bob. To son JOHN FARRIS and two
daus JANE ANTHONY and FRANKEY MARTIN each 25 cents.
The remainder of my estate to my son JOSIAH FARRIS
and dau PATSY PENN to be equally divided between
them. Appoint son Josiah and grandson William Penn
exor.
Wit: George Penn, Joseph Stovall, John D. Banks.
Exor Josiah Farris with sec. George Penn, Joseph
Stovall, Henry Clark.

II:97 Inv est JOHN SHACKLEFORD and HENRY SHACKLEFORD
Ret Jan Ct 1813.
Est John Shackleford: negro Clayton, Matrilda, Davy,
Ciller, Lucy, Bob T:1768.18.

Est Henry Shackleford: negros Tom, Bany, Lucy..T 706.8.4.
By Joseph Martin, Jonathan Stone, Daniel Caraisy???

II:98-99 Acct Sales Est MARTHA WALLER 5 Aug 1813 Ret Aug Ct 813
To: Lewis Jones, Francis Cox, Adam Thomerson, Archelus Hughes, Joseph Martin, Joseph Bouldin, John King, Reuben Hughes, James Dyer, Ambrose Edwards, Brice Edwards, James McCullough, Pendleton Burgess, James Devin, Joseph Barrington, Joel Dyer, David Petty, David Dyer, Carr Warrin, Barna Wells, John Burgess.

II-99-100 Inv JAMES HOPPER Ret Feb Ct 1813.
Horse, stock, furniture, tools T $287.90 by Charles Cox, William Norman, Cornelius Cayton.

II:100 Inv REUBIN NANCE 11 Mar 1813 Ret Apr Ct 1813
Blacksmith tools, miscl..T $51.32 by Joseph Martin, Alexander McCullough, John King, Benjamin Jones

II:100-102 LWT MARTHA WALLER 16 Nov 1810 Pr July Ct 1813
To BRICE EDWARDS my nephew, a tract of land and still. To my sister OLIVE EDWARDS negro Polly and my wearing apparel. To MARTHA EDWARDS a negro Matilda. To CARR EDWARDS negro Zelpha. To SUSANNAH WALLER negro Eliza. To SARAH MATILDA WALLER dau of Carr Waller and Elizabeth Waller negro Sarah. To CARR WALLER books. To BRICE MARTIN my nephew negro Richardson. To SARAH HUGHES my niece negro Henrietta. To my friend THOMAS CUSON of Spotsylvania County Fifty pounds. What remains of the estate is to be equally divided between AMBROSE EDWARDS my nephew and POLLY MARTIN my niece dau of my brother Joseph and Susanah Martin his wife.
Appoint Carr Waller and Brice Edwards exors.
Wit: A. Hughes, James Devins, David Harfield.
Archelaus Hughes, James Patterson, Jesse Martin sec for Carr Waller and Brice Edwards exors.

II:103 Acct est JOHN SMITH Ret Dec Ct 1813 with Sarah Smith and James Smith exors.
Pd: James Garland, John C. Parrish, Maj. Redd, John Coltrell, expense for bringing negro Tom from Montgomery Co., to James Smith a legatee ..T $548.16.

II:104 Inv est JACOB FARRIS Ret Nov Ct 1813
Furniture, horses, negro Boy, Bob, Daniel, stock, tools T 1021.75.

II:105-107 Inv est JOHN SMITH Ret Dec Ct 1812
Negros: Celia, Joe, Davey, 4 horses, yoke of steers,
cattle, hogs, sheep, crop of corn, tools, 500# hemp,
furniture T 2123.90. by John Waller, John Stone,
George Dillard.

II:107 Inv est WILLIAM JENKINS Ret Dec Ct 1812.
Shown us by Oliver Jenkins..furniture, sadddle, corn
T. 11.10.3 by Philip (x) Anglin, Joseph (x) Rea,
James Moore.

II:108 Acct DAVID WITT Ret Oct Ct 1813
In acct with John Witt exor.
Pd Eli Watkins, George Hairston, Thomas Jamerson,
Thomas Harbour, Thomas Hill, James Garland and John
Witt for two years service.

II:109 Acct JOHN EAST Ret Aug Ct 1813
In obedience to a Court Order Nov 1809 to settle the
accts with Thomas East Admn.
Pd Col. George Hairston Sept 1803; guardians for
Samuel M. Cole, William Dillen, D. Pannel, Thomas
Bouldin, Nathaniel W. Dandridge, John Weaver, John
Rowland Jr, George Gilmer, Samuel Carr for the
coffin for the deceased. T:143.11.6.

II:110-111 Accts CHARLES ROYSTER Ret Oct Ct 1812
In acct with William Birchett executor.
Pd: Legacies to ELIZA HATCHER, MARY HASKINS, REBECCA
YANCY and PETER ROYSTER. Trip to Lynchburg to make
settlement with Samuel Irvine. Pd Peter Gearheart,
to William Birchett for going from Mecklenburg to
Richmond to collect Irvin's draft on John
Cunningham, Thomas Dix & Co, Luke Adams, Thomas
Pace, William Hale, Henry Aistrop, Joseph Hobson,
John Alexander, John Dabney, N.W. Dandridge, Robert
Hairston, BANISTER ROYSTER a legatee.
Rec: Samuel Irvine, Thomas Dix, John Cunningham.
We, N.W. Dandridge, P.H. Fontaine, Joseph Hopson
appointed to settle the accounts of William
Birchett Admn of Charles Royster have examined the
documents..twenty three pounds for William J.
Royster we think the account should be credited five
pounds to Elizabeth Hatcher, Mary Haskins, Rebecca
Yancy and to Banister Royster fifty pounds.

II:112 Acct DAVID WITT Ret Oct Ct 1811
Pd taxes, Widow Witt, Thomas Harbour, Sarah Witt,
"Thomas Harbour by wish of Thomas Jamerson's Bond",
Philip Anglin, Bhill? Anglin, William Smith, Eli
Watkins, John Trent, George Reid, James Moores
exors, David Mays, John Witt acting exor.
Rec: Philip Anglin, James Larrimore, Archibald
Farris, Thomas Jamerson.

II:113 Dower of SUSANNAH MARTIN Ret Feb Ct 1811
George Hairston, Thomas Starling, Benjamin Jones
appointed to allot dower to SUSANNAH MARTIN widow of
JOSEPH MARTIN..350 acres near Leatherwood Crk.

II:113-114 Inv est MARTHA WITT Ret Jan Ct 1812.
The estate which came into the hands of MARTHA WITT
at the decease of her husband JESSE WITT.
285 gal cyder, 25 gal brandy, horse, corn, flax,
oats, deduct a colt sold at a sale. T:33.12.6 by
John B. Trent, Archelaus Farris, John Stone.

II:114 Acct THADIUS SALMON Ret Mar Ct 1811
In acct with John Salmon admn. Pd George Hairston,
Richardson Herndon, Luke Adams, John Redd. Accts
dated from 1802 to 1810.

II:114 Inv WILLIAM MOORE 6 Dec 1811 Ret Jan Ct
1812
dates: 1807-1810. Bonds on Peter Garland, Thomas
Dix & Co, Joseph Williams by David Mullins, Thomas
Jamerson, Robert Anderson.

II:115 Inv est WILLIAM MOORE Ret June Ct 1811
By Robert Anderson, Thomas Jamerson, David Mullins.
Negros: Bob, Dick, Phillis, Tom, Agga, Tammy,
Sterling, 5 horses, wagon, still, livestock,
furniture T $2980.00.

II:116 Acct JESSE WITT with John Waller admn of
MARTHA WITT who was the executor of JESSE WITT.
Ret Jan Ct 1812
Pd: William Dillon, Reuben Long, John B. Trent, John
Smith, John Waller, A. Horney for Joel Witt. To
WILLIAM DILLON one-third part; to REUBEN LONG
one-third part; John Waller, A. Horney for JOEL WITT
his third part..the whole being divided by consent
of the legatees.

II:117 Inv est THOMAS FOSTER Ret Apr Ct 1812
Furniture, tools, horse, cattle, sheep T $134.15 by
Thomas Eggleton, Benjamin Dyer, Joseph Garrett.

II:118 Acct JOHN HEFFLEFINGER Ret Sept Ct 1813
Pd Thomas Dix & Co, Capt John Pace, N.W.Dandridge,
Dr. William Hereford, John Hefflefinger, Henry
Hefflefinger, Polly Franklin, Alexander Bouldin,
David Mason.

II:119 Inv JOSEPH MARTIN 6 Jan 1812 Ret Jan Ct
1812
Negros Tom, Cuff, Sall, no T. by Joseph Jones, Davis
Petty, Ambrose Edwards.

II:119   Inv ARCHIBALD HATCHER   Ret Oct Ct 1812
Cow, mare, furn and plantation tools T26.2.4 by John
Waller, William Brewer, Thomas Nicholas.

II:120-123 Sales est JESSE WITT Ret Jan Ct 1812
27 Oct 1810 to Samuel Hill, John Bailey, William
Brewer, Reuben Long, William Hill, Thomas Cheatham,
John Waller, John H. Trent, James Kington, Zebedu
Weaver, Archibald Farris, John Rea, Henry Fee, John
Salmon Jr, John Stone, Dev. Jarrett, David Lanier,
Richard Watson, William Dillen, William Brown, John
Waller, Archibald Morris, Dr. Trent, Henry Clinton,
Lewis Hensley, Nathan Shelton, Thomas Bouldin Jr,
Abner Rea, Aaron Mills, William Morris, Thomas East.
T257.4.6.

II:123   Sales JESSE WITT estate 4 Nov 1809 Ret Jan
Ct 1812
To John Weaver, D. Trent, R. Lee, Henry Clinton,
Reubin Long, Samuel Hill, John Bailey, William
Mills, James Shelton, P. Shelton. T:34.19.10.

II:124-126   Inv REUBEN NANCE   Mar 1812 Ret Apr Ct
1812
Negros: George, Moses, Peter, Robin, Rachel and
children, Jane, Isaac, Ben, Will, Jane and children,
Disie and children, Easter, Jerry, Martin, Simon, 6
horses, stock, furniture, church bible, plantation
tools, wagon T:1937.3.9 by Joseph Martin, John King,
Alexander McCullough.

II:127 LWT JAMES OAKES 23 July 1804 Pr 25 Feb 1805
Lend to my son JAMES OAKES the land whereon I now
live on Smith River being 226 ac m/1 which I
purchased of William Price, to have and hold during
his lifetime then to his heirs which I give unto
them. I give the land I have on the south side of
Smith River, 124 ac m/1 the land opposite the other
tract, with all real and personal property to be
equally divided among the following children: BETSY
HOPPER, SALLY PULIAM and POLLY GOODWIN. To my son
LABAN OAKES twenty five pounds. To my son HEZEKIAH
OAKES twenty five pounds.   To my son JOSIAS OAKES
one dollar.
Wit: William Harrison, Isaac Potter, Rowland
....bly, Levy Burton.
Appoint as exors James Hopper, William Pulliam and
Joseph Goodwin.
Thomas Nichlas, Thomas East and William Norman sec
for exors.

II:128   LWT JOHN NICHOLAS   25 Jan 1805 Pr 31 Mar
1806
-weak in body--To my son JOHN NICHOLAS the property
he received when he left me. To my son THOMAS

NICHOLAS SR by my first wife the part he received
when he left; to dau ANN BURNS the part she
received; to son DAVID NICHOLAS the part he
received; to my eldest grandson JOHN NICHOLAS,the
oldest son of my son JOHN NICHOLAS, a horse; to my
grandaughter CAROLINE MATILDA NICHOLAS the tract
whereon I now live, bed, furniture, 2 cows and
calvs, 2 sows and pigs. To Silvy Loving the young
woman that lives with me, a bed, furniture, cow,
calf, sow and pig. To my son THOMAS NICHOLAS JR son
of my last wife, all the rest of my estate and he is
to serve as executor.
Wit: John Dillard, Elizabeth (x) Lanier
29 Sept 1805 William Hill and Robert Allen sec for
Thomas Nicholas Jr.

II:129 LWT JOHN BURGESS 14 Nov 1805 Pr 26 July 1806
-in a low state of health in body--
To my son DAVIS BURGESS one dollar.
To my dau ELIZABETH HEWLETT one dollar.
To EDWARD D. HEWLETT ten pounds.
To POLLY M. HEWLETT ten pounds.
To NANCY D. HEWLETT ten pounds.
To my dau MARY A. BURGESS a horse and saddle, cow
and calf, bed and furniture and to live at home as
long as she remains single.
To my wife MARY BURGESS during her natural life or
widowhood, all my estate both real and personal.
To my son JOHN BURGESS all of my estate at the death
or marriage of my wife, and to be the executor.
Wit: Thomas East, William East, John Mattox.
Thomas East and John Rowland sec for exor.

II:130-132 LWT EDWARD DELOZEAR Sr 31 May 1805 Pr
29 Dec 1805
-weak in body..to my son JESSE DELOZEAR five
shillings; to my son ASA DELOZEAR five shilling. To
my wife ANN DELOZEAR the remainder of my estate both
real and personal during her lifetime and at her
decease the personal property to be divided equally
between my son EDWARD DELOZEAR and dau RHODE
DELOZEAR. After the decease of my wife my dau RHODE
to have 100 ac across the lower end of my land from
Lomax line to my son JESSE'S line. The upper part,
plantation and 300 ac to my son EDWARD DELOZEAR.
Appoint my wife executor.
Wit: George Phillips, John Burch Jr, Sarah Burch.
29 July 1805 Hancock County, Georgia
John Burch Jr and Sarah Burch do testify that Edward
Delozear did sign, seal and acknowledge the said
Will.

II:132 LWT MICHAEL WATSON 23 June 1805 Pr 23 Feb
1807
-weak in body.. Exors to be John Davis Sr and

Nicholas Akins. To my eldest dau NANCY EGGLETON one shilling. To my grandaughter JANE DAVIS 30 ac being part of the tract where I now live, to be taken on the Chestnut Fork of Leatherwood Crk. The remainder of my estate to be divided among the rest of my children: DAVID WATSON, MARGARET GRIGGS, JOHN WATSON, REBECCA DAVIS, JANE AKINS, ROBERT WATSON, SAMUEL WATSON.
Wit: Vincent Wyatt, Adrian Anglin, William Shackleford.
Joseph Bouldin and Benjamin Jones sec for exors.

II:133-134   LWT JOHN ZACHARY   10 June 1806 Pr 28 July 1806
-very sick and weak--
To CATY VAUGHN and MARTHA VAUGHN her daughter, all my stock of cattle, hogs, household and kitchen furniture and all other property to me belonging to be equally divided between them. Appoint Markham Lovell and Caty Vaughn exors.
Wit: William Heard, Thomas Garner, Elizabeth (x) Vaughn.
George Hairston sec for exors.

II:134-135   LWT SUSANAH DILLEN 6 May 1819 Pr 8 Nov 1819
-in a low state of health-
To my sister ANN WASHINGTON kitchen and house furniture. To my sister ANN WASHINGTON, SOLOMAN WASHINGTON, GEORGE WASHINGTON, JOSEPH CARTER DILLEN and LITTLEBERRY DILLEN my negro woman Frances, stock of cattle and hogs and all other property to be sold and equally divided between the first legatees named to wit: ANN WASHINGTON, SOLOMAN WASHINGTON, GEORGE WASHINGTON, JOSEPH CARTER DILLEN, LITTLEBERRY DILLEN. Out of the sale of my property my executors shall pay unto JOYCE DILLEN for her attendance on me $20.00 prior to the division. Appoint John Salmon Jr and Soloman Washington exors.
Wit: John Salmon Jr, William F. Mills, William A. Taylor.
Daniel Prillaman, Charles Smith sec for exors.

II:135-136   LWT BRICE MARTIN 21 Dec 1818 Pr 8 Mar 1819
To my wife all the real and personal estate during her natural life and to have the liberty to dispose of negro Chaney.
To my son JOSEPH MARTIN negros Will and his wife Winney and children Tom, George, Mary, Mayor and Sarah. At the death of my wife, I give to the heirs of my deceased son WILLIAM MARTIN negros Bob, Judah and Nann. after my wifes decease my land is to be sold and the money divided between my son JOSEPH MARTIN and the heirs of my deceased son WILLIAM

MARTIN. The perishable estate, after my wifes decease, to be sold and divded to above mentioned heirs. Appoint Thomas East and John Barksdale exors.
Wit: John Turner, Mary (x) Turner, Nancy (x) Turner.
George Hairston sec for exors.

II:136-137 LWT WILLIAM DRAPER SR 25 Jan 1816 Pr 13 Apr 1818
Lend unto wife FRANCES DRAPER during her natural life or widowhood negros: Bob, Marget, Peggy, Jane and all my land, stock and furniture, plantation tools..and at her decease to be sold and divided among my children or their heirs. To my son ASA DRAPER five shillings and the rest of the property divded equally between my three sons: JOHN DRAPER, WILLIAM DRAPER, THOMAS DRAPER and my grandson JOHN WESLEY DRAPER. Appoint sons William Draper and Thomas Draper exors.
My grandsons part to be kept by the executors until he becomes 21 yrs of age.
Wit: James Bradberry, Michael McDonald, Tabithia Bradberry.
Henry Clark and Francis Murphy sec for exors.

II:137-138 LWT THOMAS WILSON SR 19 July 1816 Pr 9 June 1817
To my son JOHN WILSON during his lifetime 50 acs, part of the tract where I now live and a mare. To son JAMES WILSON the tract where I now live, subject to the life estate which I have given to my son JOHN WILSON. Also to my son JAMES negros Charlotte and Jack. To my dau NANCY WILSON wife of AARON WILSON 5 negros:Sarah, Mourning, Arch, Jim and Daniel. To my son MOSES WILSON negros Sarbry and Reuben. To my dau SIBLEY GILLEY wife of GEORGE GILLEY negros Rhode, Milly and Sally. To my son THOMAS WILSON one dollar. To my dau WINNEY REA and PATSEY BRASHEARS each one shilling. I give to the representatives of my dau POLLY GILLEY and BETSY JASON deceased, one shilling. The residue of my estate to my sons JAMES WILSON and JOHN WILSON equally. Appoint sons James and Moses Wilson as exors.
Wit: N.W. Dandridge, Ealy (x) Bryant, Allen Smith.
George Gilley, William Bays and George Hairston sec for exor James Wilson.

II:138-139 LWT FRANCIS COX 17 Jan 1812 Pr 13 Jan 1817
-weak in body- To my dau ELINOR GRAVELY negros Jerry, Will, Polly, Lucy, Oulila. To dau ELIABETH OLDHAM negros Jude and Joe, 100 ac on the north side of a branch..The balance of my land, 100 ac m/l to my dau ELINOR GRAVELY. The stock, furniture and

remainder of the estate to be sold and money equally divided between two daus ELIZABETH OLDHAM and ELINOR GRAVELY. Appoint George Hairston and Francis Gravely as executors.
Wit: Benjamin Dyer, John Conaway, George Gravely.
Benjamin Dyer sec for George Hairston.

II:139-140 LWT JOHN BECK 8 Apr 1818 Pr 14 Sept 1818.
-weak in body- To my wife ANNA BECK all the property that was hers at our marriage with my stock, house furniture to her and her heirs. I give my negro Charles and my money in Tenn. about $700.00 and my claim to a certain tract of land on the Tennessee River entered in the name of John King to be equally divided between my brother ROBERT BECK and my three sisters: THEADOCIA HOLLAND, MARY FURGASON and JUDEA BURNETT. My desire is for my wife to give unto NANCY SCALES a horse worth between $75. to $80.00. Appoint my step-son PETER D. SCALES my executor.
Wit: George Hairston, Robert Hairston.
William C. Bouldin sec for Peter D. Scales.

II:140-141 LWT WILLIAM HAYS 17 June 1806 Pr 13 June 1816
To my wife SARAH HAYS all my estate both real and personal during her natural life with the power to dispose of any part she should consider a benefit to the estate. My youngest son PETER HAYS will live with and care for his mother during her life in consideration of his dutiful services my will and desire is: I give to said son PETER HAYS all property that is in the possession of my wife at her decease. Appoint sons John and Peter Hays as executors.
Wit: Peter Dillard, John Dillard Jr
Peter Dillard and Philip Hays sec for Peter Hays.

II:141 LWT JESSE ATKINSON 15 May 1812 Pr 14 Mar 1814
To my wife RUTH ATKINSON all my estate real and personal during her natural life and negro Alex to dispose of as she thinks proper. The residue of my estate I give to my four single daus: ELIZABETH, BECKEY, RUTH and SALLY to be equally divided between them. To my son ISAIAH ATKINSON, after decease of my wife, the tract of land whereon I now live provided he complies with the conditions of an agreement entered into and respecting the said tract and deposited in the hands of John Dillard. Should he die without issue before my wife, then my wife is to dispose of said property for the benefit of the children. Should any dau marry before the decease of my wife, they are to receive a cow and calf, bed and furniture. The other children who have left me

and furniture. The other children who have left me have received property namely: STEPHEN ATKINSON, WILLIAM ATKINSON, SOLLAMAN ATKINSON, JESSE ATKINSON, JOBB ATKINSON and daus NANCY GILL, now deceased, and POLLY MOORE.
Appoint wife Ruth Atkinson and son Isaiah Atkinson and John Dillard exors.
Wit: John Dillard, J. P. Hill
John Dillard Sr and Jesse Atkinson sec for exors.

II:142-144   LWT JAMES BAKER SR 13 Jan 1820 Pr 14 Feb 1820
Wife SALLY BAKER all my estate both real and personal during her lifetime or widowhood. To my son JAMES BAKER the tract of land whereon I now live. To my son DANIEL BAKER a part of my Going tract on Blackberry Crk near the place where my son JEREMIAH BAKER lives during his lifetime or should he marry and have issue then to them. Should Daniel die without issue the land to be sold and divided among the other five children. The executors to reserve 1/5 part of the personal estate, after the other legacies, for DANIEL BAKER, should he marry and have heirs to them, if not to be divided among other five children. To son JEREMIAH BAKER the land whereon he now lives. To JEREMIAH STONE one dollar. To my grandson DANIEL STONE negros: Joana, Nathan, Tilda, Becky, Godfrey, Cathy and Burwell, should he die without issue to the other heirs. To dau ELIZABETH ROWLAND negros: Patt, Chany, Mann, Ralph and $100.00. To dau POLLY STONE 1/5 part of the personal property but to remain in the hands of the executors and be managed by them, at her decease to her children except Daniel Stone. To my other three children:JAMES BAKER, JEREMIAH BAKER and JEMIMAH BAKER an equal part of the balance of my personal estate. To my son JEREMIAH BAKER negro Esther. To the children that I have lent negros viz: James Baker negros Nance, Eliza and Pressy; Polly Stone negro Milly; Jeremiah Baker negros Ele and Keziah; these are to be brought forward upon the distribution and added to the rest of the estate to be divided among:JAMES BAKER, JEREMIAH BAKER, JEMIMAH BAKER and POLLY STONE.
Appoint wife Sally Baker, Jeremiah Baker and Col. John Dillard exors.
Wit: John C. Traylor, John Morris, William F. Abington, Thomas Nunn.
John Pace, Thomas Baker, James Baker Jr, Daniel Stone, John P. Hill and German Baker sec for exors John Dillard and Jeremiah Baker.

II:144-147   LWT   HENRY LYNE   5 Nov 1806 Pr 26 Jan 1807
My mulatto woman FANNY O'CONNER and her four children: PATSEY HARRIS, MARY ANN HARRIS, EMALINE

HARRIS and FANNY O'CONNER HARRIS are to be liberated and go free after my decease and the children to be under the direction and care of my nephew HENRY LYNE of North Carolina and he is to give them schooling sufficient to have them read and the expense to be paid out of my estate. I give to FANNY O'CONNER one hundred pounds cash to be placed with Henry Lyne to be given her in sums of $20. or $30. as she may need, also a horse, 2 cows and calves, 2 sows, 8 shoats also meat and bread to her and the children for one year or as long as they stay on my plantation. The tract of land whereon Thomas Starling and myself now live to be divided viz: give the upper part of the tract to my nephew THOMAS STARLING with negros: Ned, Patunee and 4 children, George, Sally, Charles, Hannah, Eady, Boy and Daniel, cattle. To my nephew HENRY LYNE the lower part of the tract including the plantation whereon I now live and negros: Phillis, Peter, Jubiler, Polly, Willis, old Peter, Anthony, Betty, Will, horses, cattle, sheep and furniture. A Deed of Trust has been given David Anderson & Co on 1800 ac, part of the before mentioned tract..not sure of what is owed, legatees to pay proportional part. I empower my nephew HENRY LYNE to receive from the executors of my deceased brother JOHN LYNE the balance of money due me as per his Last Will. Henry Lyne also to sell my land lying in the Western Country left me by my brother EDMOND LYNE,deceased. I have a free born negro lad named WALLIS HARRIS bound to me by Overseers of the Poor, I desire at my death Thomas Starling take him and keep him until he is 21 years of age. Appoint Henry Lyne and Thomas Starling executors.
Wit: John Cox, John French, Catherine S. French, Samuel (x) Fodrell.
Codicil 5 Nov 1806
I desire Henry Lyne to lend my horse Dart to his mother during her life and at her decease to my nephew EDMUND LYNE.
Wit: John Cox, Samuel (x) Fodrell, John French, Catherine French, J. Gregory.
Thomas Dix, Samuel Hill, John B. Trent, H. Fontaine and Thomas East sec for exors.

II:147-149 LWT CHARLES ROYSTER 1 Feb 1805 Pr 24 June 1805
In a low state of health..To wife ELIZABETH ROYSTER the land where I now live, 1200 ac, during her natural life and lend 15 negros: Billy, Joe, James, Jimstone, Humphrey, Sawny, Ephraim, Sally, Washington, Letty, Moses, Jack, William, Celia and Robin also lend my stock and household furniture, at her decease as hereinafter directed. To my dau MARY HAWKINS five pounds.

I bequeath the land I own in Mecklenburg County, 260
ac m/1, be sold by my son-in-law WILLIAM BIRCHETT
and one half of the money from the sale to my
grandson WILLIAM ROYSTER son of GEORGE
ROYSTER,deceased. To ELIZABETH ROYSTER,dau of
George Royster, CHARLES ROYSTER son of George
Royster and GEORGE ROYSTER son of George Royster
each five pounds. The residue of the money I leave
to be disposed by the exors. To my grandson WILLIAM
ROYSTER negro Will. I bequeath to be sold negros
Harry, Hannah, Patience, Kakee, Nelly, Rogerton and
Charles and the money applied as follows: to my son
BANISTER ROYSTER fifty pounds; to my dau REBECCA
YANCY five pounds. After the decease of my wife,
the land whereon I now live, 1200 ac, to be sold. To
my son PETER ROYSTER five pounds cash. I bequeath
to my Executors in trust for the benefit of my son
PETER ROYSTER and his children the value of 100 ac
of land when sold and the interest to go towards
support of said son and children, also in trust for
them negros Gilbert and Ailsye. When the youngest
child of said Peter come of age the whole of the
property be equally divided among his children. To
my dau SUSANAH TRAHERN the value of 150 ac of land
when sold and negros: Critt, Bobb, Stillar, Frank,
Randolph, Edmund and Susannah. To my son BANISTER
ROYSTER the value of 100 ac. To my grandson CHARLES
YANCY the value of 100 ac. To my dau ANN BIRCHETT
the value of 100 ac. To my son EDWARD HOWE ROYSTER
negro Frank and the value of 350 ac when sold. To
my dau PATSY COLEMAN ROYSTER the value of 300 ac
when sold. After the decease of my wife I give unto
my son EDWARD HOWE ROYSTER and my dau PATSY COLEMAN
ROYSTER the 15 negros lent my wife, stock,
furniture, plantation tools and all property lent my
wife.
Appoint wife Elizabeth Royster, William Birchett and
Joseph Hopson exors.
Wit: William Hereford, Reuben Alexander, Joseph
Boudlin Jr.
Codicil: The 5th item in the within relative to a
tract of land in Mecklenburg County it is my desire,
after sold the money to be equally divided between
the children of my son GEORGE ROYSTER, dec'd by
name: WILLIAM J. ROYSTER, ELIZABETH ROYSTER, CHARLES
ROYSTER and GEORGE ROYSTER. dated 7 March 1805.
Wit: Reuben Alexander, Henry Aistrop, Samuel Hester.
George Hairston and Samuel Hester sec. for exors
Elizabeth Royster and William Birchett.

II:149-150 LWT WILLIAM FRANCIS 27 Jan 1814 Pr 11 Jan
1814..A letter written by said William Francis which
serves as his Will.
"January 27th 1814 Dear Sister...I received your
letter dated January 10th 1814 which I was happy to

hear that you was well and I am happy to inform you that I have mended very much and I am in Hopes that I shall meet you and all my friends and relations once more in Henry. There is some talk of our being discharged the 10th of March and I expect to get home by the first of April if I live. Sister it appears from your letter that you have most of my property in your possession and if I never return home Sister Judy you must keep what you have in possession. Sister Polly may keep what she has got except the land and the balance she has got you must settle in what I owe. Sister Judy if you have not received that money from Mr. Hill you need not do anything until I return home. If I should die you must collect the money and keep it. You must pay sister Sally three or four dollars out of the money you get from him. Capt. Shelton and his Company are generally well. If I never return you must pay Old Redd what I owe him and that don't exceed 15 shillings and you must pay sister Sally and Polly what I owe them. After paying them you may have the balance sister Judy. In the letter I received I understood when Stone heard that I was dead he was going to keep my horse. Stone must keep my horse until I return home unless you hear for certain that I am dead, and then you must go and get him Sister Judy and keep him. You must tell John Kernal and family that I think hard of him that he has never wrote to me where he lives. Remember my love to him and family, remember my love to Mrs. Reamy and Mrs. Hunter and Mr James Rea and all his family and to John Hefflefinger and all the family and to James Robertson and his family and to John Burgess and family and to Davis Burgess and his family. I am dear sister your most affectionate brother till death. William Francis.
Ret 11 July 1814, Henry Co Court.
John Pace sec for Judy Francis.

II-151-152   LWT   HENRY SHACKLEFORD 31 Oct 1805 Pr 27 Jan 1806
-weak in body- Lend to my wife MARY SHACKLEFORD during her natural life or widowhood all the land and plantation where I now live with the house furniture, stock and negros Rose, James and Sail.
To SUSANNAH JACOBS ten pounds, a cow and calf and colt. To my son HENRY'S children one hundred pounds and after the decease of my wife, they are to have the balance of their part in money when my land is sold. To my son HENRY SHACKLEFORD five shillings in case Henry should want the care of the children's money, he is to give security. I leave my wife's part to be equally divided among my four sons and my son SAMUEL'S children namely: JOHN SHACKLEFORD, JAMES SHACKLEFORD, WILLIAM SHACKLEFORD, DANIEL

SHACKLEFORD and LUCE SHACKLEFORD. The balance of
the estate not given to be equally among my four
sons JOHN, WILLIAM, JAMES and DANIEL and my son
SAMUEL'S children after deducting twenty pounds for
my son JOHN and fifteen pounds for my son SAMUEL'S
children. Appoint my son JOHN SHACKLEFORD as exor.
Wit: Samuel Marshal, William Martin, Francis Cox.
William and Daniel Shackleford sec. for John
Shackleford.

II:152-153   LWT CHARLES DAVIS 6 Mar 1803 Pr 27 July
1803
-sick and weak-
Lend unto wife ANN DAVIS property, real and personal
of every part during her life or widowhood.
To son MOSES DAVIS one shilling.
To dau RACHEL DAVIS one shilling.
To son ISAAC DAVIS one shilling.
To dau LYDIA MURPHY one shilling
To son JOSHUA DAVIS one shilling.
To dau ELENOR DAVIS a feather bed and furniture,
dishes, cow and calf.
To son BENJAMIN DAVIS feather bed and furniture,
gun, dishes.
To THOMAS BLACKBURN DAVIS bed and furniture, dishes.
To PETER DAVIS the tract of land where I now live,
by estimate 155ac also 6 1/4 ac purchased of Joseph
Towlin and conveyed to Shadrack Dent, gun, furniture
and dishes.
To dau ANN DAVIS bed, furniture, dishes.
When my wife either marries or dies, the personal
estate to be divided as follows: equally divide
between my sons: BENJAMIN DAVIS, THOMAS BLACKBURN
DAVIS, PETER DAVIS and dau ANN DAVIS. Should Peter
die without issue then the land to be divided
between sons Benjamin and Thomas. Appoint wife Ann
Davis exor.
Wit: John Salmon Jr, John Redd, Mary Marridy.
Shadrack Dent and John Cahill sec for Ann Davis.

II:154-155   LWT JOHN HEFFLEFINGER SR 24 Dec 1808 Pr
27 Dec 1809
To my wife MARY HEFFLEFINGER all the estate both
real and personal and at her decease the executor to
sell the whole of my estate and divide it among all
of my children. The executors to be trustee for my
dau ELIZABETH ROYER'S part and no part for the
benefit of her husband JOHN ROYER. Appoint my wife
Mary and three sons George, John and Jacob
Hefflefinger exors.
Wit: William Hereford, N. W. Dandridge, John Reamy.

II:155-156 LWT ANDREW REA

31 May 1806 Pr 26 Jan 1807

-sick and weak-
To dau NANCY PAYNE negro Cela and the other property she has received.
To dau BETSY WHITLOCK negro Joshua, cow and calf with the other property she has received.
To dau SALLY NORMAN negro Lucy with the other property she has received.
To wife SARAH REA the land I now possess and negros Adam, Peggy, Patty and half of the stock, furniture, tools, grain etc during her natural life or widowhood.
To son JOSEPH REA negro Bobb.
At the decease of my wife part lent to her to be divided among my four sons: WILLIAM REA, DAVID REA, JOHN REA and JAMES REA.
Appoint sons John and Joseph Rea exors.

John Dillard sec for John Rea.

II:156-157   LWT LEONARD CHEATHAM JR 3 Mar 1815 Pr 9 Oct 1815
-sick and weak- To my wife JANE CHEATHAM all my estate during her natural life except for the provisions hereafter mentioned for my six children.
I desire my estate to be kept together for the use of the family and education of my children and as they come of age to receive a good negro, horse, bridle and saddle, bed and furniture. If my executor thinks it best for my sons to bind them out to such trade as they think best.
After the decease of my wife the land to my three sons and the personal estate to all the children.
Appoint John Dillard Jr and Peter H. Dillard exors.
Wit: John Dillard, Joseph C. Weaver, John Weaver.
Joseph Bouldin Jr sec for Peter Dillard and Jane Cheatham.

II:157-159   LWT THOMAS NUNN SR 21 Oct 1805 Pr 12 Feb 1816
-sick and weak..To my dau POLLY PACE the land on Rock Run Crk 30 ac, bounded by Newsom Pace, James Fifer, Hickerson Barksdale. To my dau DOSHA STONE one dollar. To my dau BETSY MANNER twenty five pounds. To my son THOMAS NUNN 150 ac on Rock Run Crk. To my son JOHN ALEXANDER NUNN 125 ac on Rock Run Crk and negro Jacob. To my son JOSEPH NUNN 100 acres. To my grandson THOMAS STONE 100 ac m/1 on Smith River and the waters of Rock Run Crk that joins Stephen Stone and a colt. To my son JOHN A. NUNN bed and furniture, horse.
The remainder of the estate to be divided between my sons THOMAS and JOSEPH and negros Pegg and Squire.
Appoints sons: Thomas, John A. and Joseph exors.
Wit: John Cox, William Hale, Stephen Stone.
John Dillard, Green Bouldin and Charles Smith sec

for Thomas and Joseph Nunn.

II:159-160   LWT   PRESTON   KENDRICK 28 Nov 1814 Pr 10
July 1815
-very sick and weak. To my wife SARAH KENDRICK all
my land, stock, household goods during her natural
life then to fall to GABRIEL ROBERTS provided he
takes care of said SARAH KENDRICK during her
lifetime.
Wit: Cornelius Cayton, Joseph Goud, Samuel Lowe.

II:160-161   LWT   DAVID   WITT   29 Mar 1807 Pr 27 June
1808
To JOHN WITT and BENJAMIN MOORE negro Jack.
To ABNER MOORE negro John.
The above named negros are to remain in possession
of my wife SARAH WITT during her natural life. The
balance of the estate to my wife to dispose of as
she thinks proper. Appoint John Witt and Benjamin
Moore exors.
Wit: John Dillard Jr, Thomas Harbour.
George Hairston sec for John Witt.

II:161   LWT   THOMAS   DICKERSON   6 Nov 1806 Pr 29 Feb
1808
sick and weak..Wife JEMIMA DICKERSON the estate both
real and personal during her natural life and at her
decease to be divided among the children. Appoint
sons JOHN DICKERSON and WILLIAM DICKERSON exors.
Wit: Barna Wells, John Wells, Henry Lawrence
Barna Wells sec for John Dickerson.

II:162 LWT JESSE WITT   16 May 1809 Pr 25 Sept 1809
To wife MARTHA WITT all of the estate for her
natural life. To grandson GEORGE DILLEN land whereon
I now live after my wife's decease. To grandson
DAVID WITT, son of JOSEPH WITT, a colt, bridle and
saddle. To JESSE WITT LONG, son of NANCY LONG,
negro Andrew.
Whatever else that remains after the decease of
Martha Witt to be divided between my children: JOEL
WITT, TABITHA DILLEN and NANCY LONG. My two
children in Georgia DAVID WITT and ELIZABETH
RICHARDSON have had of my estate all I intended.
Appoint wife Martha Witt as exor.
Wit: John Waller, Joseph Bouldin Jr
John Waller sec for Martha Witt.

II:163 LWT ARCHIBALD HATCHER SR 2 June 1812 Pr 13
July 1812
To my grandchildren, the heirs of NATHAN SHELTON,
WILLIAM DURHAM and ARCHIBALD HATCHER JR all my land
where I live to be sold when WILLIAM HATCHER, son
of ARCHIBALD HATCHER JR comes of age and the money

divided between the heirs above mentioned. I do grant my son Archibald Hatcher Jr and Nathan Shelton the privilege to cultivate and live on the land and divide the profits therefrom until WILLIAM HATCHER comes of age. Executors to sell what is necessary to settle debts and the balance to my son ARCHIBALD HATCHER. Appoint John Dillard exor.
Wit: W. A. Taylor, James Shelton, Francis Shelton.
James Shelton sec for John Dillard.

II:163-165   LWT   REUBEN   NANCE   10 Jan 1812 Pr 9 Mar 1812
weak in body..To wife NANCY NANCE negro Benn, cow and calf, bed and furniture to dispose of at her discretion. To wife Nancy for her use during her natural lifetime or widowhood negros: Isaac, Dyder, Will, Hester, Jury, Martin, Simon, Joe and Janey also a wagon and team, still, all plantation tools, cattle stock, land, plantation house, furniture and the mill. My desire is that my old stock of negros should be divided between my oldest family of children that I had by my first wife viz: Son WILLIAM NANCE, deduct $175.00 pd him, son BIRD NANCE, son ALLEN NANCE, son CLEMENT NANCE, son JOSEPH NANCE, daus MARY CROUCH, SUSANAH MCCULOUGH and TABITHIA SHACKLEFORD the following negros: Bess' children, George, Peter, Moses, Bob, Rachel, Jiney and Gill. As to my son ISAAC NANCE, son JOHN NANCE, son REUBIN NANCE, son ISHAM NANCE and Dau SARAH SANDFORD I have given each of them their part as follows: son Isaac has received one hundred pounds; son Isham one hundred pounds; son John received negro Amy; dau Sarah Sandford a negro named Liza; son Reuben negro named Lucy. The balance of my estate to my last children: STEPHEN NANCE, PEYTON NANCE, SARAH PHILPOTT, EDMUND NANCE, LESSONLA NANCE, NANCY NANCE and REUBEN SAUNDERS NANCE. Appoint Benjamin Jones as exor.
Wit: John Conaway, Edward Richardson, John Lovell.
Thomas Starling, Joseph Gravely Sr sec for Benjamin Jones.

iI:165-166   LWT   EDWARD   H. ROYSTER 12 Dec 1809 Pr 29 Jan 1810
weak in body..Give unto WILLIAM BIRCHETT of Mecklenburg County one half of my estate during his natural life and at his decease to be equally divided among the children of my sister NANCY BIRCHETT. The other half of my estate to JOHN TRAHERN during his lifetime then to children of my sister SUSANNAH TRAHERN. Appoint William Birchett and John Trahern as exors.
Wit: William Hereford, Joseph Hopson, John Reamy.
William Hereford and Thomas Dix sec for exors.

II:166-167 LWT STEPHEN CARTER 28 Sept 1806 Pr 30 Mar 1807
--in a low state of health
To wife MARGARET CARTER land, plantation where I now live and personal estate during her lifetime. At the decease of my wife land to be sold and equally divided between my six sons: NATHAN, ABRAHAM, THOMAS, STEPHEN, JOHN and WILLIAM CARTER. The personal property divided between daus LIZA SNELL and LUCY HOLT.
Appoint wife Margaret Carter, Abraham Carter and Benjamin Woodson as exors.
Wit; Martha Lesnen?, Edward (x) Poston, Elizabeth (x) Alexander.
George Hairston sec for Margaret Carter and Abraham Carter.

II:167-168 LWT WILLIAM MOORE 19 Oct 1810 Pr 12 Nov 1810
-aged and infirm- To my wife ELIZABETH MOORE during her natural life all my land laying off for my son JAMES MOORE 200 ac that joins Thomas Hill and Anul? Rogers. My daus to have same privlege as my wife as long as they remain single and grandaughter MATILDA MOORE the same privilege as long as her remains single. To my dau ANN MOORE negro Tom, to SALLY MILLS negro Patrick, horse and cow; to my son WILLIAM MOORE land in Patrick County, horse, cow and my other land after the decease of my wife and the marriage of his sisters and niece. Negros Bob and Dick to son WILLIAM MOORE after my wife's decease. To my dau BEDDY negro Fanny; to my grandson WILLIAM MOORE negro Sterling; to my son ELECK MOORE $1.00; to my dau BETSEY WILSON $1.00.
Appoint wife ELIZABETH MOORE as exor.
Wit: David Mills, Joseph Allen, James Dillard.
Peter Garland and William East sec for Elizabeth Moore.

II:168 LWT SAMUEL MARSHALL 30 Sept 1809 Pr 14 May 1810
To my wife CASANDRA MARSHALL, after debts are paid, personal estate to dispose of as she thinks proper with the following exceptions: to my son BENJAMIN MARSHALL bed and furniture after my wifes decease or sooner if she wishes; to dau NANCY bay mare at decease of wife; to grandson BENJAMIN MARSHALL my rifle gun; to my grandson SAMUEL MARSHALL my shot gun. I lend unto my wife the land and plantation where I now live during her natural life. At her decease to be sold and divided among my children; SALLY ARNOLD, LEWIS MARSHALL, DENNIS MARSHALL, NANCY MARSHALL, BENJAMIN MARSHALL, SUSANAH BARROW, JOHN MARSHALL.
Appoint son Dennis Marshall, Elisha Arnold and John

King exors.
Wit: John King, Thomas Hailey, Anderson Hagwood.

II:169-170 LWT HENRY JONES 28 July 1801 Pr 9 July
1810
-weak in body-
In 1791 I divided the estate I had and gave half to
the five older children viz: JOSEPH JONES, FIELDING
JONES, ARMSTEAD JONES, MILDRED JONES and LEWIS
JONES. They had half the livestock, negros Clay,
Stephen, Sall, Terry, Ben and Sall and 4 horses.
I lend unto my wife SUSANAH JONES the whole of my
estate I now possess, also the tract adjoining
Samuel Shoemate with all the negros and other
personal property. I give unto my other four
children viz: WINNEY JONES now WINNEY ALEXANDER;
PETER JONES, WILLIS JONES and DELILAH JONES the
balance of my estate.
Appoint wife Susannah Jones and Samuel Jones exors.
Wit: Clement Nance, William Nance, Mary Nance, John
Cox, George Hairston, N.W. Dandridge.
William Jones, George Hairston, Lewis Jones sec for
Joseph Jones.

II:171-173 Inv est JESSE WITT 26 Sept 1809 Ret Oct
Ct 1809
Negros Cate and Andrew, livestock, furniture, tools
T 1151.43 by John B. Trent, John Stone, Gregory
Durham, Archibald (x) Farris.

II:173-174 Acct est JOSEPH ANTHONY 29 May 1809
In acct with Joseph Anthony Jr
Pd John Cox, William Willis, Randolph Adams, William
Dillen, Jonadab Wade, George Hairston, Jacob Farris,
Joseph Jones, John Philpott, Samuel Anthony, Fleming
Saunders, Benjamin Jones, Nathaniel Clabourne, Adler
Agee, John Redd, David Taylor, Elizabeth Anthony,
Thomas Dix, Joseph Phyfer, Zachariah Philpott,
Thomas Clark Bouldin, Benjamin Dodson, Peachy R.
Gilmer, William Anthony, William Dillen, Littleberry
Dillen.

II:174-175 Inv est WILLIAM MARTIN Ret Oct Ct 1809
By John Philpott, William Turner and Charles Smith.
Cattle, hogs, wagon, horses, negros: Dorcas, Selah,
Esther, Manuel, Tiller, Rachel, Sephy, Alisey,
tobacco, furniture..No T.

II:175 Inv est TERRY HUGHES 24 Feb 1810 Ret Mar Ct
1810
Negros: Charles, Citter, Polly and children,
Jeffrey, horse, furniture, livestock..T $1779.91. By
David Mullins, Robert Allen, Joseph Allen.

II:176-177 Inv est EDWARD H. ROYSTER Jan Ct 1810

Negros: Billy, Robin, Jimston, Jack, Heank, William, America, Sally and children, George, Letty, furniture, livestock T 1111.6.6. By John Reamy, N.W. Dandridge, P. H. Fontaine, Joseph Hopson.

II:177-178 Acct DAVID WITT 23 May 1809 Ret June Ct 1809
In acct with John Witt, exor. Payments and receipts from July 1808 thru Apr 1809 to: Benjamin Moore, Thomas Harbour, John Dillard Jr, Edward Watkins, John Harbour, William Smith, Samuel Saunders, Jesse Corn, John Trent, George Hairston, Sarah Witt, Sarah Harbour, John Witt.
Signed: James Baker Sr, John Philpott, Jesse Carter.

II:178 Acct WILLIAM GRAVES Oct 1806 Ret Mar 1808
In acct with Joseph Anthony exor..payments to Luke Adams, John Dabney and for Taxes.

II:178-179 Acct HENRY SHACKLEFORD Ret Apr Ct 1808
In acct with John Shackleford exor
Payments for 1806: Thomas Dix, John Degraffenauter, Francis Northcutt, Mrs. Oldham, Samuel Shackleford, Joseph Barrington, Christopher Robertson, James Sheilds, Joseph Martin, John Shackleford.
Received of Thomas Dix for sale of tobacco

II:179-180 Inv DAVID WITT 20 Aug 1808 Ret Aug Ct 1808
Negros: Lydia, Thenia, John, Lack, furniture, tools, horses..no T.
By Thomas S. Hill, Edward (x) Watkins, Philip (x) Anglin.

II:181-182 Inv est BALDWIN ROWLAND 20 Apr 1809 Ret May Ct 1809
Furniture, 7 horses, livestock T120.14.2 by John Cahill, James Murphy, John P. Pyrtle, James Meredith.

II:182-183 Inv est THADIUS SALMON Mar Ct 1810
As produced by John Salmon Sr, furniture, livestock T70.2.3.

II:183-185 Inv JOHN DAVIS Nov 1807 Ret Feb Ct 1808
Furniture, plantation tools...no T.
By A. Hughes, George Dyer, Elijah Richardson.

II:185-186 Inv JESSE HEARD 15 Mar 1809 Ret Mar Ct 1809
Furniture, livestock, tools, negros Christopher, Mark, Ann and Judy. T.485.12.7 by William Warrin, Robert Pedigo, John Jamerson.

II:186-187 Inv JOSEPH MARTIN 16 May 1809

N.C. currency, Bonds on the following: Hopkins, Williams & Wortham; Barna Wells, Terry Hughes, A. Hughes, B. Martin, W. Mills, G. Martin, Johnson, Harlin, J. Martin.
Signed: Joseph Jones, ---Petty.

II:187 Acct ISHAM HODGES 27 June 1808
In acct with Robert Hodges exor.
Two days at Widow Dickersons and Woods; Pd Franklin Co; Caleb Tate, James Callaway, Andrew Patterson. Robert Hodges, exor of Isham Hodges, sold the tract where said Isham Hodges lived containing 600 ac to John Clay husband of Elizabeth Clay late Elizabeth Dickerson; Josiah Dickerson and Robert Dickerson. 22 June 1808.

II:188 Inv JOHN ROWLAND 21 Dec 1807 Ret Jan Ct 1808
Negros: Prince, Lude, Hanner, Lett, Bob, Delse, Platt, Major, Squire, Lug, Nancy, Peter. Furniture, wagon, Tools, Livestock T 993.9.9. By Sanford Reamy, Thomas East, Peter Garland, Ruben Payne.

II:189-190 Dower of JANE ANTHONY Oct Ct 1809

Report of the dower (1/3rd part) to Jane Anthony widow of Joseph Anthony: negros Daniel, Nancy, Davie a horse and colt, Livestock, furniture, still, Plantation tools T 388.3.4.
By John Salmon, George Waller Jr, Benjamin Jones, George Hairston.

II:190-191 Inv SAMUEL MARSHALL 31 May 1810 Ret June Ct 1810
Livestock, furniture, tools, horse T $265.66 by Dennis Lark, George (x) King, James Howard.

II:191-192 Inv JOHN HEFFLEFINGER 10 Jan 1810
Furniture, livestock, tools T. 161.4.4 by Joseph Hopson, Sanford Reamy, John Reamy, P. H. Fontaine.

II:193 Acct JOSEPH ANTHONY 14 Feb 1810 Ret May Ct 1810
Pd taxes 1808-1809.
Received of Thomas Rogers.

II:193-194 Sales est THOMAS STOVALL 3 Jan 1807 Ret Feb Ct 1808
Sales to: Benjamin Simmons Jr, James Savage, William Robertson, John Weeks, John Jett, John Moreland, George Stovall, David Kelly, Reubin Herndon, Robert Jenkins, John Robertson, Isaiah Paslur, Henry Graybill Sr T 3681.87.
Hancock Co. Ga. 7 Jan 1808 The above is a true copy of the original acct of sales. Signed: Myles Green.

II:194 No. I 18 Mar 1807
Received of Joseph Cooper, Myles Green and Bolling
Hale for distribution to the heirs of the estate of
Thomas Stovall brought to the state of Georgia by
Elizabeth Stovall, adm of said estate. Heirs:
Joseph Stovall, Polly Stovall, Pleasant Stovall.
T:1973.51.

II:195 No. 2 18 Mar 1807
Received of the above named $657.33 in full of my
distribution share of my father Thomas Stovall's
estate brought to George by my mother. signed:
George Stovall. Witness: John Ingram.

II:195 No. 3, 18 Mar 1807
Received of the above named $657.33 in full of my
share in right of my wife Sally, orphan of Thomas
Stovall, of the estate taken to Georgia by Elizabeth
Stovall. Signed: Benjamin Simmons.

Ii:195 No. 4, 18 Mar 1807
Received of the above named $657.33 in full of the
share of Ruth Stovall of the estate of Thomas
Stovall taken to Georgia by Elizabeth Stovall.
Signed: John Weeks, guardian for Ruth Stovall.

II:195-196 The above receipts were received and
recorded. John Weeks married the widow Elizabeth
Stovall.
Clerks Office, Hancock Co, Ga. 7 Jan 1808.

II:196-199 Guardian Acct of SAMUEL M. COLE by Joseph
Alexander. 22 Jan 1807 Ret 20 June 1808.
Expenditures and receipts of the following:
David Lanier Sr, Thomas Nunn, George Hairston, John
Trahern, Peter Anderson, Luke Adams, Joshua
Farrington, William Nunn, Thomas Pace, William
Reamy, Sanford Reamy, William Banks, Thomas
Williams, David Lanier Jr, Joseph Williams, Joseph
Trahern, Robert Allen, John Rea, Reubin Payne,
Joseph Hobson, Thomas East, Thomas Dix & Co, David
Custer, Susanah Adams, John Lanier, N. W. Dandridge,
William Pace, Collin Moore, Elisha Phillips, Joseph
Alexander, William Callaway, Edward Royster, R.
Wilson, Capt. John Salmon, Parks Bailey, Philip
Ryan, Abner Rea, Charles Hatcher, William Hale,
David Mason, Frederick Eckolds, John Cox, Robert
Anderson, Mrs. Reamy, William Nunn.

II:200 Acct JESSE WITT Nov 1809 Ret Dec Ct 1810
In acct with John Waller, admn.
Sold horses to Joel Witt; a negro willed to Jesse
Long, Horse, saddle, bridle for Jesse Witt. Notes on
John Christian and John Leake. Yearling to H.
Clifton. Receipts of: Dr. Banks, Dr. Hunter, John

Owens, Dr. Hereford, William F. Mills, Dr. Dillen, Dr. Trent, George Hairston, Nathan Harris, Reuben Long, William Dillen and Joel Witt.

II201 Division of estate and accts of JOSEPH ANTHONY 2 Nov 1809
Division of negros:
To Betsy Anthony negros Milly and Sally.
To Samuel Anthony negros George and Jim.
To John B. Gilliam negro Judy.
To Joseph Anthony negro Jack.
To William Anthony negros Betty and Dolly.
To Jacob Anthony negro Cela.
To Josiah Anthony Negro Fanny.
To each legatee bonds included total of 111.7.1.
Accts: Bouldin & Hunter, Maupin & Meredith, Robert James, B. Woodson, William Lovell, William Holt, Fortune P. Bouldin, Thomas Graves, Green Bouldin, Isham Nance, J. Cahill, Pyrtle & Rowland.

II:202 Acct EUSEBUS STONE Ret 29 Aug 1810
In acct with Susannah Stone, Admn.
1798 payments to: John Cox, George Hairston, Bartlett Wade, Micajah Stone, Eusebus Stone, Richard Stone.
Recd: John Barksdale, James Martin Sr, John Wade, James Quarles, Jesse Carter, Littleberry Dillen, William Witt, Newsom Pace, George Key, Josiah Turner, Robert Woods, Thomas Jett, Richard Stanley, John Salmon, David Ross, Richard Stanley, John Salmon, William Draper, Thomas Boulding, Robert Hunter, Daniel Ross.

II:203-204 Inv WILLIAM BREWER 6 Apr 1815 Ret May Ct 1815
Negros: Rachel, Phiney, furniture, tools, livestock T:$1017.30 by Hubbard Hatcher, George Dillard, Henry Bington.

II:204 Acct DAVID WITT Ret Oct Ct 1815
In acct with John Witt. Paid Clerk, Sheriff and George Hairston.
Signed: Thomas Nunn, James Baker, Jeremiah Baker.

II:205-206 Inv ELIZABETH GOIN Ret Mar Ct 1816
Livestock, furniture, Household effects, plantation tools T:$546.78 by John Morris, James Baker Jr, Guy Smallman.

II:207 Inv WILLIAM HEARD 7 Mar 1816 Ret Mar Ct 1816
Negros: Adam, Mary, Kite, Adam, Ciss, 4 horses, furniture, livestock T:$2570.74 by Samuel Philpott, John Turner, Peter Smith.

II:208-211 Inv GEORGE WALLER Nov 1814 Ret MayCt 1815

Negros: Jinney, Matilda, Mime, Linda, Ralph, Lita, Tom, Will, Ben, Gabriel, Jim, Milly, Aimy, furniture, horses, grain..no total. By James Baker, Burwell Bassett, John Salmon Jr.

II:211-212 Inv JONATHAN LYLE 10 Oct 1815 Ret Dec Ct 1815
Negros: Patience, Betsy, Billy, Malinda, tools, horses, livestock T:$1109.55 by Jabez Gravely, Henry Lawrence, William Lawrence.

II:212-213 Inv SHADRACK DENT 11 Jan 1815 Ret May Ct 1815
Livestock, horses, furniture T:326.74 by Henry Clark, James Murphy, John Cahill.

II:214 Acct WILLIAM R. JENKINS 31 May 1816 Ret June Ct 1816
In acct with Oliver Jenkins, admn.
Pd: George Hairston, Thomas Jamison, Henry Clinton, Mary Jenkins.
Recd: Sales and rent from John Trent for 1814.

II:214-215 Acct JOHN STOKES Ret Nov Ct 1815
In acct with Benjamin Jones exor.
Bonds on Bowman & Co and Peter Garland.

II:215-219 Sales est GEORGE WALLER 23 Jan 1815 Ret May Ct 1815
To: E. Waller, George Waller, William Spencer, Green Bouldin, J. Redd, J. Burris, Jeremiah Baker, James Baker Jr.
Dr. Trent, Hardin Hairston, James Bolin Jr, Mrs. Ozbourn, J. McCraw, Ben Smith, Henry Kington, J. Bailey, Samuel Hill, William Graves, William Hanby, William P. Adams, John Salmon, J. Nance, William McCraw. T:1277.11.10.

II:219-221 Inv CHARLES ROYSTER 13 July 1805 Ret July Ct 1805
Negros: Billy, Will, Joe, Harry, Jameston, Humphrey, Ephram, Robbin, James, Swaney, Washington, Moses, Jack, Billy, Frank, Rochester, Sally, Letty, Cila, Hannah, Betty, Rachel, Patience, Milly, Chance; livestock, riding chair and harness, plantation tools, furniture T:2441.9.0 by P. H. Fontaine, N. W. Dandridge, Thomas Dix, Eliza Royster, William Birchett.

II:222 Inv REUBEN NANCE 10 July 1815 Ret July Ct 1815
Tobacco to Lynchburg by Stephen Nance; tobacco sold to Edward Staples..Bonds and accts on: Jesse Crouch, John Lovell, Fleming Thomerson, Isham Nance, Joshua Compton, Alexander McCullough, Benjamin Dyer,

William Compton, Arnold Thomerson, Eliza Royster, James Barrington, Cairy Numan, John Flemon, Joseph Gravely, James Grigg, Barna Wells, William Kimbro, Thomas Hailey, Simpson Cesser, John Conway, Richard Griffin, John King son of George King, William Hale, William Tooms, Vincent Wyatt, Jesse Simpson, Arch. Hughes, Stinson Watson, Francis Northcutt, Preacher King, Thomas Dix, Isham Nance T:143.3.10. By: Joseph Martin, John King, Alexander McCullough.

II:223 Acct REUBEN NANCE Sept 1814 Ret Sept Ct 1815
To settle with Benjamin Jones admn.
Vouchers   275.0.9
To legatees   724.5.7
To Widow   237.0.4
Appraisement of estate 2095.14.11.

II:223-224 Inv WAYLAND PAYNE 29 Nov 1815 Ret Dec Ct 1815
Furniture, livestock, tools T:$214.34 by Reuben Payne, John Quarles, Thomas Nunn.

II:224-226 Inv SAMUEL HILL 9 Nov 1815 Ret Dec Ct 1815
Furniture, tools, negros: Tennessee, Sopha, Moriah, Saunders, Betty, Booker, Harriett, Betty, Winny, Easter, Robin, Jaba, Parker, tobacco, corn, horses, livestock..no T. By John Waller, John Dillard Jr, John B. Trent.

II:226 Inv EDWARD LEWIS Ret June Ct 1815
A total of 35.11.0, but does not list property.

II:226-228 Acct RALPH SHELTON 24 Nov 1814 Ret Aug Ct 1815
In acct with Eliphaz Shelton.
July 23, 1789, Bond 9 yrs interest; tax 1785-1789; pd Pittsylvania Co. tax, John Redd; Tax for 1786; Pd Clerks Ticket for citing the decedant levy free; Coffin and winding sheet; Col. Hughes; Moorman Lauson (Lawson?); Bread corn for widow and 3 children one year; Same for widow and 4 children 3 months; 9 months board for 2 children Capt. William Carter; John Henderson; Alexander Askin in Amalia County; board and schooling for one boy, a legatee 5 years 6 months; James Shelton; John Davis; James Harrison; Winding sheet for Mrs. Shelton; Interest on the 10 pounds pd James Harrison from 1764 to 1789, 25 years.
Received money from sales and from rent of the plantation from 1790-1794.

II:228 Inv LEONARD CHEATHAM 6 Nov 1815 Ret Nov Ct 1815
Negros: Pleasant, Sophia, James, Nancy, Saler,

Mariah, Milly, Miles, Matt; furniture, horses, livestock, grain, tobacco, Bond on Dr. Stovall due Aug 1816. By: Isiah Atkinson, William Clinkscale, John Weaver.

II:228-230 Sales est MARTHA WALLER 1 Dec 1813 Ret Dec Ct 1814
To: Brice Edwards, Reuben Hughes, Benjamin Dyer, Madison Hughes, Carr Waller, Jonathan Stone, Ambrose Edwards, Davis Petty, Joseph Barrington, David Dyer, Willis Jones, William Hereford, George W. Sinoot, Godfrey Burnett, Joel Dyer, Barna Wells, Thomas Dix, John Devin, Dabney Waller, James Hailey Sr, Jesse Martin, John McMillion, Joseph Martin, Lewis Jones, Nathan Woodall, David Burton, Henry Edwards, Arch. Hughes. T:$401.23.

II:230 Inv PETER LEAK 24 June 1815 July Ct 1815
Shown us by Hannah Leak, admn.
Negros: George, Doll, Jany, Meala, Zada, Sam; furniture, livestock, cotton machine T:$2040.60 by John Rea, Henry Fee, Phillip Hays.

II:231 Division est JOHN SHACKLEFORD Ret Dec Ct 1815
Jane Woodall, late Jane Shackleford wife and relict of John Shackleford, has chosen negros Bob and Matilda as her third part..there being ten heirs and seven slaves (Davy, Clayton, Kitty, Reubn, Siller, Charlotte and Lucy) we can make no further division. We are of the opinion that the other personal estate can be better divided by sale.
Signed: Joseph Martin, Christopher Robertson, Davis Petty.

II:231-233 Inv JAMES OAKES 7 Oct 1815 Ret Dec Ct 1815
Furniture and a cow T: $81.20, by William Hewlett, William Chauarny??
7 Oct 1815 sales of the estate of James Oakes $109.65 with Hannah Oakes admn.

II:233-234 Inv WILLIAM FRANCIS JR 3 Sept 1814 Ret Oct Ct 1814
Horse in the hands of Jonathan Stone; furniture; shoemakers tools; Bond on Peter Garland; Note on William Taylor; note on James Rea Jr T:$131.37. By Sandford Reamy, William Reamy, David Burges.

II:234-235 Inv COL. HENRY LYNE 26 Jan 1807 Ret Dec Ct 1807
Stock, furniture, tools, 5 horses, tobacco, riding chair, harness and cushion; negros: Jupiter, Anthony, Peter, Will, Young Peter, Fanny and 4 children, Phillis, Betty. No T by John Cox, P.

Garland, P. R. Gilmer.

II:236-237 Sales JOHN EAST Ret Oct Ct 1814
To: John Quarles, Joseph East, Peter Garland, George
Hairston, Francis East, David Rea, John Mattox,
Randolph Adams, Robert Anderson, John Rea, William
East, William Dillen, Reuben Payne, Leonard Rea,
Joseph Martin, Langston Pace, Thomas Pace, Joel
Pace, Thomas East. T:364.12.10.

II:237-238 Inv BURWELL BASSETT 14 Mar 1816 Ret May
Ct 1816
Horses, cattle, sheep, hogs, tobacco, furniture,
tools, negros: Isbell, Jane, Susan, Chana, Charles.
Bonds on William Spencer and John Carter due
1809-1811. By: George Waller, John Waller, J. P.
Hill.

II:238-239 Inv HENRY DILLEN 10 June 1814 Ret June
Ct 1814
Horses, livestock, furniture, negros: Gin, Alse,
Betty, Phill, Joe, Sam, Phillis, Eltra, Anica,
Winney, Bboker, Jacob T: $3265.40 by Burwell
Bassett, Samuel Hill, John B. Trent.

Inventory of the estate of MARY DILLEN 10 June 1814
T:$9.75 by the above appraisers.

II:240 Inv JAMES TAYLOR Ret Nov Ct 1814
livestock, horse, furniture, tools and cash in the
hands of Thomas Cheatham T:$121.00 by Joseph Rea,
George Martin, Henry (x) Fee.

II:241 Acct WILLIAM MOORE 7 Apr 1814 Ret June Ct
1814
At the house of Elizabeth Moore to settle the
accounts current of the estate of William Moore.
Pd taxes 1811-1813; Dr. William Banks, Fleming
Saunders,attorney; Joseph Rea, Frank Dabney, Dix &
Co; P.R. Gilmer, attorney; Archibald Farris.
T:$207.61.

II:241-242 Inv WILLIAM HAYS Ret July T 1814
Livestock, horse, furniture, negro Jack T:$576.66 by
James Rea, George Martin, Henry (x) Fee.

II:242-243 Sales JAMES TAYLOR Ret Sept Ct 1814
Sales of the estate of James Taylor at Mrs.
Elizabeth Taylor's.
To: Joseph Atkinson, Madison R. Hughes, Henry Fee,
Elizabeth Taylor, Capt. G. Penn, Josiah Reid, John
Hughes, Elijah Gray, Hudson Martin..No T.

II:243-244 Acct JOHN MARSTIS Ret Nov Ct 1804
In acct with James Marstis admn.

11 Dec 1798 pd the following legatees:
Thomas Marstis, Jacob Marstis, Adler Agee, John Edens, Elizabeth Marstis, James Marstis, Elizabeth Marstis Jr.
Pd George Hairston, Peter Garheart, tax for 1798-1799. T:79.5.8. Admn: Joseph Anthony and Joseph Bouldin.

II:244 Inv JESSE ATKINSON 8 Apr 1814 Ret Apr Ct 1814
Negro Abel, furniture, livestock T $852.91 by Joseph Rea, Phillip (O) Anglin, Leonard Cheatham.

II:245 Inv NATHAN SHELTON 4 May 1804 Ret May Ct 1814
Horse, livestock, furniture T:$169.43 by John Waller, George Dillard, William Brewer.

II:245-246 Inv JAMES SHELTON 2 June 1814 Ret June Ct 1814
Furniture, negros: Grace, Jack, Winney and 6 children, $174. in cash, cattle, no T..by John Dillard Jr, Thomas Nicholas, Henry Abington.

II:246 Inv MERDITH PEIRSON Ret Apr Ct 1805
Total 18.19.0 by Joseph Gravely, John Davis, Nicholas Akin.

II:247 Acct ELIZABETH WEBB Ret 3 May 1805
In acct with John Pace, admn 1805
pd burial expense; Dr. William Hale.
Bonds on: John Smith, John Baley, Joseph Terry, William Dillen, William Long, John Carnil, John Wilson, Hezekiah Dunn. Tobacco sold to William Ramsey.
Elizabeth Webb was the executrix of Merry Webb dec'd.

II:247-248 Acct MERRY WEBB Ret July Ct 1805
Bond on James and Aron Wilson for the hire of negros Jane and Robin after the death of Elizabeth Webb.
1778 funeral expense.
1779 pd Col. Thomas Dillard by John Cox.
1805 Pd John Dabney 6 days to Buncombe (N.C.?)

II:248-249 Inv GABRIEL STULTZ Feb Ct 1805
Horse, other livestock, furniture T:50.2.0 by Samuel Marshall, William Roberts, John Wills Sr.

II:249 Inv ANN NICHOLDSON Ret 26 Feb 1805
Furniture, clothing items T:13.17.7 by James Howard, William Stokes, Henry Clark.

II:250-251 Acct SAMUEL M. COLE Jan 1804
In acct with John Alexander, guardian.

1 Jan 1803 rent pd Sandford Reamy, John Pace, Samuel
Corn.
Hire of negros to: James Rea, William Hereford, Mary
Miller, Sally Harrison, Henry Carter, Henry Clark,
Isham Nance, Terry Hughes, John Alexander, Richard
Rea, John Mattox, Robert Anderson.
Pd: George Hairston, John C. Cox, Joseph Hopson,
John Worsham, Hugh Nisler, Thomas Dix & Co, Peter
Garland, Francis Cox, Frederick Eckolds, John East,
Luke Adams, Sally Harrison, Robert Anderson, N. W.
Dandridge, ...Taylor, William Nunn, William Dillen,
Capt. Jett.

II:252 Inv HUGH ONEAL 13 June 1805 Ret June Ct 1805
Horse, tools T:6.17.6 by Thomas East, Robert
Anderson, William East, John Wash.

II:252-253 Inv ELIZABETH WEBB jj8 Mar 1805 Ret May
Ct 1805
Negros: Robin and Jane, furniture, tobacco T:102.4.3
by John Quarles, Joseph Terry, William Dillen.

II:253-255 Inv HENRY SHACKLEFORD Ret Apr Ct 1806
Negros: Jack, James, Charlotte and children, Billy,
Bob, Lucy Barber, Billy Taylor, Joh, Patsey Winston,
Rose, Sally Walker, Billy Aenet, Judah and 2
children, Tom, Vassey and 2 children; furniture,
cattle, plantation tools, horses T:1447.11.0 by
Samuel Marshall, John Wills, Francis Cox.

II:255 Inv JOHN ZACHARY Ret 6Sept 1806
Livestock, furniture T: 14.15.3 by William Heard,
James Murphy, ---Williams, John Jamerson.

II:256 Sales JOHN ZACHARY Ret 6 Sept 1806
Sale of furniture and livestock T:17.9.11.

II:256 Acct JOHN STOKES Ret Nov Ct 1804
Joseph Anthony, Jacob Farris, Carr Waller to settle
accounts with Benjamin Jones, exor.
Bonds on Spears Brown & Co, Peter Garland and Thomas
Jones.

II:257 Inv PETER HUNTER 5 June 1805 Retd July Ct
1805
Negro Dick, 2 horses, livestock, furniture, hemp,
rye, his part of land sold by the executors of
Alexander Hunter dec'd. T:236.13.2 by John Cox,
James Baker, Samuel Philpott.

II:257-258 Acct MORDICA HORD 21 June 1805 Ret 24
June 1805
To William Hord for 2 trips to S.C.; judgements
against Gen. Sumpter of South Carolina.

II:258 Acct   THOMAS STOVALL Ret Sept Ct 1805
In account with Joseph Stovall and Elizabeth
Stovall.
Pd: George Hairston, William Banks, Thomas Jamerson,
Charles Cox, Peter Leak, James Officer, Josias
Taylor, Robert Anderson, James Larrimore, Charles
Thomas, John Weaver.
Receipts: James Officer, George Hairston, Joshua
Haynes, Col. Lyne, William Heard, William Read,
Tunstall Cox, John Harris, Archibald Farris.

II:259-260 Division estate of JOHN EAST Ret Oct Ct
1814
Peter Garland, Thomas Graves and Robert Anderson are
appointed to settle the accounts with Thomas East.
To Widow Frances East, her dower, 72.13.5. To Joel
Pace, John Mattox, Joseph East, David Rea and Thomas
East 29.1.4 each.

II:260 Division estate of HENRY SHACKLEFORD Ret Feb
Ct 1807
To John Shackleford negros Lucy and Bob.
To William Shackleford negros Sam, Judy, America and
John and five pounds from the heirs of Samuel
Shackleford.
To the heirs of Samuel Shackleford negros Tom,
Vassey and Susa.
To James Shackleford negros Jack, Charlotte and
Henry and to pay Daniel Shackleford twenty five
pounds.
To Daniel Shackleford negros Betty, Taylor and
Patty.
Division by Joseph Martin, Samuel Marshall, William
Hale.

II:261 Inv JOHN NICHOLAS Ret 24 Jan 1807
Furniture and livestock T:77.0.6 by Garrot Williams,
Archibald Farris, David Mullins.

II:261 Acct JOHN P. PYRTLE Ret 18 Oct 1806
In account with John P. Pyrtle admn.
Two days moving the property home, 2 yrs schooling
Joseph and Arn ??; boarding family, clothing.

II:262-263 Inv JOSEPH ANTHONY Ret 30 Mar 1807
Negros: Daniel, Betty, Faney, Jack, George, Polly,
Nancy, Cela, Judy, Milly and Dave, furniture, 6
horses, livestock, tools..no T. By Benjamin Jones,
George Waller, Charles T. Philpott. Joseph Anthony
and Jane Anthony admn.

II:264 Acct PHILIP BRASHER 7 Jan 1805 Ret Mar Ct
1806
In account with Robert Brasher.
1802 Bonds on William Dillen, Phillip Counes ?,

81

Abijah Hughes, Henry Dillender. Notes on William C.
Rea, Nathan Carter.
Sales: Phil Brooks, Nancy Brasher, Winefield Roach,
Robert Brasher, Creassey Key who purchased slave of
James Brasher, Joseph Bailey a legatee of P.
Brasher.
Sold 164 ac to Philip Brasher Jr.
Pd John Waller.
Legatees who purchased at the sale: Philip Brasher;
Nancy Brasher, Winfeild Roach, Cressey Key who
purchased up the claims of James Brasher and Joseph
Bailey in right of his wife Martha, a legatee.

II:265 Inv STEPHEN CARTER Ret Nov Ct 1807
Furniture T:16.5.0 by George King, Matel Lasuere,
John Jamerson.

II: 266-269 Acct SAMUEL M. COLE Ret Jan Ct 1807
In account with Joseph Alexander formerly with John
Alexander guardian.
Bonds on: Luke Adams, Robert Lorton, Thomas Dix,
Sandford Reamy, Thomas Pace, William Mitchell, Peter
Garland, Abner Rea, Robert Anderson, John Wash,
David Lanier, Thomas Williams, Thomas Nunn, George
Hairston, John Trahern, Joseph Farrington, William
Nunn, William Reamy, William Banks, Joseph Williams,
David Lanier, Robert Atkins, Reuben Payne, Joseph
Hopson, Thomas East, David Custer, Susanah Adams.
Receipts: Peter Garland, Thomas Nunn, John Worsham,
Thomas Dix, Abner Rea, Philip Ryan, Edward Royster,
James Lanier, John Alexander, David Lanier, Thomas
Nunn, George Hairston, John Trahern, Robert
Anderson, Luke Adams, Joshua Farrington, William
Nunn, Thomas Pace, William Reamy, William Banks,
Sandford Reamy, Joseph Williams, John Trahern,
Robert Allen, John Rea, Reuben Payne, Thomas
Williams, Joseph Hopson, Thomas East, Thomas Dix &
Co, Susanah Adams, John H. Lanier, Gilbert Rowland,
John Rowland.

II:269-270 Dower of ANN WALLER May Ct 1815
Widow of George Waller, division by George Waller Jr
and John Waller Admn.
1815-negros: Will, Sunday, Lett, Jenny, a horse,
livestock and furniture T 479.18.4.

II:271-273 Acct SAMUEL COLE 28 Sept 1805
In acct with John Alexander, guardian.
Rents from: Randolph Adams, Samuel Carr, James Rea,
Abner Rea, Luke Adams, Robert Anderson, John Crouch,
John Alexander, Robert Alexander, Peter Gearhart.
Pd: William Hord, Samuel M. Cole's expense to Ky.,
James Lanier, Thomas Williams, William Hale, Thomas
Jett, Alexander Culverson, William
Dillen, Samuel H. Hunter, William Mitchell, John

Pace, Joseph Hopson, Peter Garland, Martha Fontaine, Abner Rea.
Bonds on: Sandford Reamy, Luke Adams, Robert Lorton, Peter Gearhart, William Mitchell, Abner Rea, Peter Garland, John Wash, Robert Anderson, Thomas Pace, Thomas Dix & Co, David Lanier Jr, Thomas Williams.

II:273-274 Acct BENJAMIN REA Sept Ct 1815
With George Hairston Admn
1801 - Pd Clerk of Henry Co; William Reamy, William C. Rea, Francis Cox, Russel Cox, William Francis, Reubin Payne, John Reamy, John Keene, Mildred Rea. Pd each legatee 7.18.10.
Bonds on: Milly Rea widow, John East, Thomas East, Joseph East, Wilson Rea, Benjamin Harrison, James Bowling, James Rea, William Rea, John D. Rea, John Wash, Richard Rea, John Kernal, Russel Cox, Reubin Payne, Charles Worham, George Gilley, Henry Carter, Thomas Nunn, Richard Cox.
To each legatee sum of 7.18.10, legatees:
Mildred Rea, widow
Reuben Rea
Nancy Rea
Kitty Rea
Henry Rea
Patea Rea
Sally Rea

II:274 Inv MICHAEL WATSON Mar Ct 1807
Still, livestock, furniture, no T, by Samuel Marshall, Joseph Gravely, George (x) Dyer.

II:276-277 Sales HENRY SHACKLEFORD 7 Jan 1807 Ret June Ct 1807
Auctioneer: John Shackleford
Sales to: Lewis Jones, John Conaway, William Long, George Dyer, Pendleton Burgis, James Dyer, Mary Shackleford, William Shackleford, Daniel Shackleford, John Shackleford, Joseph Martin, Joseph Barrington, Thomas Fleman, Susana Jacobs, Capt. Northcutt, Joseph Jones, Peter Thomerson, Tapley Akin, John Minter, Elias Thomerson.

II:277-279 Inv WILLIAM SHELTON 24 Sept 1807 Ret Sept Ct 1807
Negros: Bob, Sarah, Hannah, Ceila, Anica, Minta, Aron, Philip, Jack, Gena, Chany, Matilda, Washington, 3 horses, livestock, furniture T:$3093.81 by John Waller, William Hill, John Smith.

II:279-280 Inv CHARLES DAVIS 27 Aug 1807 Ret Aug Ct 1807
Furniture, plantation tools.no T
By John P. Pyrtle, William Heard, John Cahill, Juner Meredith.

II:281 Inv MARTHA FONTAINE Ret Mar Ct 1820
Books: 6 vols History of All Nations, Johnston's
Live of the Pawitz?, Roman Republic, Spirit of Law,
Byles Lectures, Burns, Travels in Spain, Blair's
Sermons, Law Books, French and Latin books, "a
parcel of old injured and odd vols", family bible,
furniture. No T, John J. Fontaine, Admn.

II:282 Inv DAVIS PETTY 28 Mar 1820 Ret May Ct 1820
Negros: James, Reubin, Aron, Edmond, Pamplett,
Tisly, Jane and children, Kitty, Charity, Marsha,
Charlotte, Milly, Wesley, Billy, Susan, Peter, Paig
Peter, Dick, Emanuel, Harry, Amuel, Garrett, David,
Hannah, Dackis, Milly, Little Hannah, Patrick,
Nelson, Coleman, Darkis, Judith, Peter. 12 horses,
livestock, tools, grain and feed, tobacco,
furniture. Bonds on: John Reamy, Richard B. Beck,
Gilbert Dier, P. H. Fontaine, N. W. Dandridge,
Richard Royal, William Motterby, John and Williamson
Milner, Perkins, Nelson Bryant, Hugh Rakes, William
Lanes, Robertson & Beavers, James Dyer, George
Warrin, George Aron, Jesse Warren, Samuel Cobb,
William Bays, William Gravely, Barna Wells, Sampson
Cheshire, John Morris, Daniel Reamy, Toliver
Shoemate, Daniel Woodall, George Hairston, Willis
Jones, Stinson Watson, William Austin and John
Conaway, James Laurence and William Austin, Leroy
Hankins and Obediah Minter, Joseph Barrington,
Richard Lyle, John Johnson, John Hankins, P. & G.
Gravely, Richard B. Beck, Christopher Robertson,
George Gravely, Edward Eans, William Gravely, John
Garrett, William Dickerson, Keziah Hamilton, Obediah
Minter, John and Isiah Morton, Jesse Warren, John
McMillen, Jesse McMillen, Gilbert Hankins, William
McMillen, Anthony D. Hadon, Benjamin Lanier, Edward
Popejoy, Joseph Davis, James Woodall, William
Martin, Spencer Coterill, Stephen Austin, Joseph
Jones, George Adams, William Ware, Obediah Owen,
Ellis Wilson, John Reamy, Thomas B. Dandridge,
Joseph Bouldin, James Nance, Samuel Lane, Jabez
Gravely, William and James Mastin, J. Scott, Richard
Booker, Isaac Morton, Benjamin Hubbard, William
Gravely, George Roberton. No T.

II:286-288 Inv JAMES BAKER Mar Ct 1820
Negros: Jula, Hannah, Sarah, Else, Charles, Fanny,
Fan (old), Ruth, Isaac, Purlina, Billy, Ralph,
Keziah, Susanah, Letty, Bob, Sarve, Edmond, Will Jr,
Jim, Jinny, Tilda, Becky, Godfrey, Cutty, Burwell,
Isaac, Alexander, Micajah, Ephriam, Madison, Ann,
Louisa, Kitty, America, Mary, Betsy, Westly, Philip,
Lucy,Patty, Mariah, Matt, Gabe, Eliza, Pussy, Nance,
Milly, Lizy, Chany. Livestock, 6 horses, tobacco,
blacksmith tools, furniture, plantation tools, Va.

bank notes, bonds against German Baker. T:$18,706.00
by John Morris, William Taylor, Landin P. Stovall.

II:288-289 Inv WILLIAM H. WOOTEN   Ret Mar Ct 1820
In acct with John B. Trent.
Bonds: John Colson, William Leake. Accts: Reuben
Kington, Hannah Leake, Thomas S. Hill, Norman
Staples, Nancy Brewer, Archibald Stovall, Henry
Morris, Pines Allen, Stith Martin, William Spencer,
Nathaniel G. Bassett, Lewis Bryant, Landis P.
Stovall, David Custer, Joseph Kington, Josiah Leake,
John Kington Sr, Samuel McCraw, George Dillard, Miss
Nancy Ozbourne, William Graves, Charles Hardy,
William Hill, Jacob Bundren, Abner Lack, Jesse
Martin, Nathaniel T. Robertson, Leonard Sheffield,
Henry G. Mullins, John Sharp, Brice Martin, William
T. Cole, James Taylor, William Smith, John Morris,
Darling Allen, Maske Bradbury, James Dyer,
Washington Rowland, George Salmon, Henry Clinton,
Clabourne Bundren, John Salmon Jr, William Fontaine,
William Lawless, Edward C. Staples, Mrs. Fontaine,
Keah Jinkins, Est. of Leonard Cheatham, James
Edmunds, Jane Wooten T:263.8.3.
By John Waller, George Waller Jr, Thomas Nicholas.

II:289-290 Inv DANIEL SMITH 14 Apr 1820 Ret June Ct
1820
Livestock, horses, tobacco, furniture, tools, no T,
by Lewis (x) Franklin, Jesse Estes, William (x)
Holt, William (x) Moore.

II:291-292 Inv JOHN CAHILL Nov Ct 1816
Livestock, horses, blacksmith tools, Negros: Peter,
Jesse, Kiah, Harry, Rocker, Primus, Will, Caty,
Fillis, Tempe, Judy, Febey, woman and child, Lucy,
woman and child in the hands of Zachariah Philpott
also horse and furniture, cattle, hogs, saddle,
pewter and horse in possession of Thomas Cahill.
T:$8605.80 by John Wills, Leonard Murphy, John P.
Pyrtle.

II:292-294 Acct HENRY and MARY DILLEN Oct Ct 1816
By John Dillard and William F. Mills.
Amount of the estate of which there is to be an
equal division amongst all the legatees $3858.25.
Pd: William P. Adams, P. R. Gilmer. To Thomas
Officer part of his legacy; Jacob Dillen part of his
legacy; pd Carter Dillen for Sally Dillen; Pd Carter
part of his legacy; pd Alexander Cook part of his
legacy. Pd William F. Mills acct; pd part of the
estate to 3 daus $255.33. Pd Thomas Bouldin, Capt
John Waller, Capt John Hughes, Maj John Redd.
20 Sept 1816 by Robert Allen, Joseph Bouldin Jr,
Thomas East.

II:294-295 Acct   MARTHA WALLER Aug Ct 1816
In acct with Brice Edwards and Carr Waller, exors.
Pd funeral expense; tax for 1813; Dr. William Banks,
Dr. William Hereford, Graneys fee, Thomas Cason,
Brice Edwards, Joseph Martin, Dabney Waller, Reubin
Hughes, Carr Waller guardian for Ambrose B. Edwards.

II:295-296 Inv   DR. WILLIAM HEREFORD 8 Aug 1816 Ret
Aug Ct 1816
Negros: Frank, Nancy, Delpha, Mary, David, Sall,
Allen, Oscar, Livina, Milly, Pugg and son Jack,
Harriett, Isaac, Charles, 5 horses, livestock,
plantation tools, furniture, medicine, tobacco
T:$6211.41 by Thomas East, Thomas Graves, Washington
Rowland.

II:296-297 Acct   GEORGE WALLER 28 June 1816 Ret Aug
Ct 1816
In acct with John Waller and George Waller Admn.
Pd Jacob McCraw a legatee   179.14.7
Pd William Waller   same
Pd John Redd   same
Pd Edmund Waller   same
Pd John Waller   same
Pd George Waller   same
Pd Clerk's ticket, Peach R. Gilmer, William P.
Adams, Hezekiah Mouldin, Archibald Farris, Edward C.
Staples, John Salmon.

II:297-298 Inv   STEPHEN MCMILLEN   3 Aug   1816
Shown us by Admn Abram McMillen.
Notes: George Dillard, Robert Pace, Joseph Cook,
David Custer, Chatten Chewning, John P. Hill,
Darling Allen; cow and calf. By George Dillard, H.
Hatcher, Darling Allen.

II:298-300 Inv   THOMAS NUNN 29 Feb 1816 Ret Dec Ct
1816
Furniture, tools, grain, livestock, negros: Squire,
Jacob, Sall, Barbary, woman and child No T, by John
Barksdale, Henry Barksdale, L. P. Stovall.

II:300-301 Inv   THOMAS REA   Ret June Ct 1820
Furniture, Horse, Cattle T:$202.75   by John Pace,
Davis Burgis, Richard Gilley.

II:301 Dower of   MARTHA REDD   Mar Ct 1819
Reubin Payne, Thomas East and Robert G. Payne allot
Martha Redd widow of Overton Redd..negros: Randolph,
Milly and Nancy also money which Maj John Redd has
to advance to make out equal half.

II:301-302 Accts   GREENWOOD BOULDIN 16 Apr 1818 Ret
Sept Ct 1819
Pd: John Reamy, Daniel Wilson, Joseph Bouldin,

Archibald McKowen, James E. Bouldin, Charles Agee,
George Hairston, Washington Rowland, Thomas East,
Absalom Morman, James Kelso, George Hefflefinger,
Thomas J. Wooten, Elisha Phillips, Francis Gilley,
William Spencer, Thomas Moore, John Wills, Joseph
Jones, Nathan Hensley, David Dyer, John Hereford,
Everton Redd, William H. Wooten, Peachy R. Gilmer,
John Redd, William Hill, Dix & Reamy.

II:303-304 Inv BRICE MARTIN 30 Mar 1819 Ret Apr Ct
1819
Negros: Will, Winny, Tous, George, Mary, Major,
Sarah, Bob, Judah, Nann, Chany, Silvy, Richmond
Silvy, 7 horses, livestock, plantation tools,
furniture, tobacco..no T. By: Reubin Payne, William
Perkins, Robert G. Payne.

II:304-306 Inv THOMAS JAMERSON June Ct 1819
Livestock, plantation tools, furniture, negros: Joe,
Darkis, America, Betsy. By George Hairston Jr,
Thomas Harbour, William East. Two inventories (1)
1237.69 (2) 1639.79, many items appear to be
duplcations.

II:306-307 Inv WILLIAM H. WOOTEN 9 Sept 1819 Ret
Sept Ct 1819
Bonds of John Colson, William Leak
Accts: Reubin Kington, Norman Staples, Pines Allen,
Nathaniel G. Bassett, David Custer, Samuel McCraw,
Hannah Leak, Archibald Stovall, Stith Martin, Lewis
Bryant, Joseph Kington, John Kington Sr, Thomas S.
Hill, Henry Morris, William Spencer, Landis P.
Stovall, Josiah Leake, George Dillard, Miss Nancy
Ozbourne, Jacob Bundrant, Leonard Sheffield, Darling
Allen, William Holt, William Fontaine, Kiah Jinkins,
William Graves, Aleus Lack Judgement, Henry G.
Mullins, James Taylor, Mark Bradley, Henry Clinton,
Mrs. Fontaine, Estate of Leonard Cheatham, Charles
Hardy, John Martin, John Sharp, William Smith,
Washington Rowland, Clabourne Bundran, William
Lawson, William Hill, Nathaniel T. Robertson, Brice
Martin, John Morris, James Dyer, John Salmon Sr,
Edward C. Staples, James Edmunds. No T, by John
Waller, George Waller, William A. Taylor.

II:308-309 Accts WILLIAM R. JENKINS 19 Dec 1818 Ret
Mar Ct 1819
In acct with Oliver Jenkins Admn.
Pd: George Hairston, Taxes, Henry Clinton, S.
Jamerson, Mary Jenkins 31 May 1816.
Sales and rent 1813, 1815 and 1816.
Pd: James Jenkins his legacy, taxes and coffin.
Signed: John Dillard, Thomas Harbour, William Moore.

II:309-311 Acct WILLIAM SHELTON Mar Ct 1819

Pd: Maj. Redd, Dr. Bradford, James Shelton, Dix, Alexander & Co, H. Lyne, Pines Allen 1807.
1816: Reuben Long, Benjamin Morris, Peter Dillard in going to Ga; William Brewer for schooling children, Greensville and Thomas Penn, Thomas Jamerson, William Hill, Blackgrove & Co, money expended going after William French in Botetourt, Thomas Nicholds, Reubin Kington, James Wade, John Shelton, John Kington, Maj Redd, Col Hairston, John Staples for tobacco to Richmond; for John going to Amherst; John Smith, John Weaver, Peter Scales, Garrett Williams, John Shelton, John Dillard.
Rec: Sale of negros: America, Hannah and 2 children, tobacco to Pines Allen, Tobacco to Richmond, 44ac sold Nicholds, bond on Rogers.

II:311   Dower of KITTURA COLE   12 Apr 1819 Ret Apr Ct 1819
Widow of the late Samuel M. Cole..Negros: Sandy ca 60yrs; Kitty 30 yrs, Jackson 9yrs, Will 6yrs, Ned 5yrs, Henry 3yrs, Maria 6yrs, Deunisa 4yrs, Taby 2 yrs, Milly 24yrs, Silva 18 yrs, Biddy 1yr, Armstead 24yrs, Rachel 50yrs, cash $166.66 her part of the value of Usley; 2 horses, cattle, part of a tract of land that has lines joining Rowland, the ford on Smith River, Reubin Payne, John Redd, Marrowbone Creek (no ac)
By: Robert G. Payne, Robert Allen, John Redd.

II:312-313 Inv FRANCIS COX   20 Jan 1817
3 horses, cattle, wagon, furniture, tobacco, corn, negros: Joe, Jude, Lucy and Dielela..no T. By Joseph Martin, James Dyer, Davis Petty.
Delivered to Joseph Gravely and Elizabeth Oldham the above negros agreeable to the LWT of Francis Cox, decd. George Hairston, exor. 20 Jan 1817.

II:313-314 Sales FRANCIS COX 21 Jan 1817 Ret Jan Ct 1819
To: William Oldham, George Hairston Jr, Milton Farny, Ambrose Edwards, Peter F. Harris, Joseph Gravely, Joseph Jones, James Dyer, Peyton Gravely, Willis Jones, Fielding Jones, Levi Cheshire, Stephen Holland, Jonathan Stone, Elijah Richardson, Barney Prunty, Toliver Shomate, John Serrate, David Hairfield, James Woodall, Barna Wells, William Creasy, George Gravley. No T.
Cash of Thomas Dix & Reamy $212.00

II:315 Inv JOHN CONAWAY   Jan Ct 1819
Furniture T: $24.65 by John King, Alexander McCulough, James McCulough.

II:315-316 Acct infant children of SAMUEL M. COLE in acct with Kittura (Kitty) Cole and William Perkins.

Jan 1819 - Feb 1820 purchase of staples (flour,
sugar, coffee, bacon) T:$79.26
Ret Mar Ct 1820

II:316-320 Acct JOSEPH MARTIN Ret Nov Ct 1817
1809 in acct with Joseph Martin, Admn
Pd: Griffin Griffith, John Cook, William Hereford in
favor of Maj Brice Martin, William Hereford for
medical service, Randal G. Adams, Samuel Armstead,
N. W. Dandridge, Robert Allen, William Nunn, David
Harfield, George Hairston, Nathaniel Harris, Joseph
Jones, Chancery Court of Richmond, Dr. William Hale,
Cash expended traveling to Tn; THOMAS MARTIN a
legatee; MRS. SUSANAH MARTIN (dower), REUBEN HUGHES
a legatee by his marriage to POLLY; costs in suit
in Tn vs Thomas Hopkins; Brice Martin for discharge
of his claim vs the Estate; PATRICK MARTIN a
legatee; George Tucker, Thomas Jackson, LEWIS MARTIN
a legatee, Reuben Hughes. Collected from Peter
Thomerson for 2yrs rent on the small plantation.
Pd Henry Edwards in favor of his wife Sarah formerly
Sarah Waller on account of a bond given Gen. Martin
by Brice Martin for the benefit of Elizabeth
Waller's children.
Rent pd to Samuel Armstead, P. H. Martin, Reuben
Hughes, Lewis Martin yearly 1809-1817.
Rec: Joseph Martin, Thomas Fluman, Abraham Williams,
William Mills, Joseph Bouldin Sr, Thomas Hopkins,
Brice Martin, Barna Wells, William Laurence, William
Hankins, Elijah Richardson, Lewis Jones.

II:320-321 Dower of MARIA WALLER Apr Ct 1818
Widow of EDMUND WALLER..no ac given, lines of John
C. Traylor, includes the dwelling house of Edmund
Waller. Signed: John Salmon, William F. Mills, J.
Dillard.

II:321-322 Inv JOHN BECK July Ct 1819
Negros: Charles, woman Phealy for lifetime of Mrs.
Beck, furniture T:$667.00.
Bonds: William French, Richard Woods, Robert Beck,
N. W. Dandridge, Frederick Beck, Jonas M. Holland,
Nicholas Scales, Joel Estes, Robert Wortham, Thomas
Gaines.
Cash in the hands of P. P. Scales. No T.
A second list by Thomas B. Dandridge, Joseph
Bouldin, William Norman.

II:322:323 Inv JOHN BAILEY Jan Ct 1818
4 negros, 12 horses, 14 cattle, 7 sheep, 3 wagons, 1
4-wheel carriage, cart, blacksmith tools, plantation
tools, 12,000# tobacco (value $1200.), 1,000#
tobacco, value $50., corn, fodder, forage, brandy,
cotton, furniture, bonds T:$4970.85 by J. P. Hill,
William Dillen, Alexander Bassett.

II:323-324 Acct WILLIAM HEARD Aug Ct 1818
Elizabeth Heard, Admn.
Pd: Lewis Davis, Forest Phifer, Peter Garland,
Littleberry Stone, Dr. Stovall, Josiah Turner, Taxes
1815-1818, Peter Smith for coffin, Samuel Philpott,
Charles Smith, Francis Murphy, John Hunter, George
Staples, Charles Smith, Thomas Nunn.

II:325-327 Inv JOHN HOLCOMB 27 Nov 1818 Ret June Ct
1818
Horses, furniture, livestock no T by Perrygin
Cahill, Juner Meredith, Ambrose Edwards.
Sales to: Joseph King, George Hairston, Benjamin
Davis, John A. Nunn, Perry Cahill, Ann Burchett,
John Fortune, John P. Pyrtle, Shors Turner, Samuel
Jamerson, John Gear, Spencer Hardy, Joseph Phifer,
William Lovell, Alexander Frazier, John Cahill,
Grimes Holcomb, Ambrose Jones..No T.

II:327-328 Dower and Allotments Est of PETER LEAKE 6
Nov 1819 Ret Nov Ct 1819
At the residence of Hannah Leake, widow, whereby
widow and all legatees agree to sell the estate and
purchase same among themselves.
Widow, 1/3rd in land taken from Manor Tract
beginning at the South Mayo River, lines of son
Peter Leake, includes the houses of her residence
reserving for son Peter a cotton patch and apple
orchard except 2 rows by the side of the road for
the use of his mother. The widow purchased negros:
Janey, Doll, livestock.
Josiah Leak the tract whereon he now lives
To Patsey Leake the Mill Tract
To Peter Leake the Rockingham Co tract
To Elizabeth negro Mealy
To Archibald Farris who md Ann Leake, negro Juda
To Nancy Leake negro Hardin
To William Leake, bed, furniture and cow
Balance left divided between the 8 children; Joseph
Leake, Elizabeth Leake, William Leake, Patsey Leake,
Archibald Farris, Nancy Leake, Peter Leake, Lucy
Leake.
By John Dillard, William Clinkscales, Joseph Rea.

II:328-329 Acct SHADRACK DENT May Ct 1818
In acct with Francis Murphy.
21 Feb 1815 sales given in by C. Bradbury.
Bonds on: Zachariah Philpott, Francis Northcutt,
Peter Thomerson, Ignatious Symms, John Conaway,
Elias Thomerson, Joseph Martin, Elijah Meredith,
Soloman Poston.
Pd: Taxes, James Murphy, John R. Salmon, J. Bradbury
and wife, J. Maupin and wife, Benjamin Dent and
wife, John Dent, William Dent.

II:329-330 Inv General Joseph Martin 27 Dec 1817
Plantation tools, livestock, horse, furniture. No T.
By Davis Petty, George Harrison, Carr Waller.

II:330-331 Sales JOSEPH MARTIN 1 Jan 1818 Ret Mar Ct
1818
Bond on: Christian & Compton; Peyton and Joseph
Gravely, Dyer & Morrison; Thomas & George King;
Waller & Petty; King & Dyer; Morten & Petty, Stone &
Stone T:$1434.75.
Following property in possession of Susana Martin
and has not been sold, furniture, horses, livestock.

II:331 Inv EDMUND WALLER Ret Mar Ct 1818
Livestock, negro Ben, furniture T $1054.75 by John
C. Traylor, John Salmon Jr, Henry Clark, Lewis
Franklin.

II:332 Acct JOHN SMITH 11 Dec 1818 Ret Dec Ct 1818
Pd: John W. Hill, Charles Farris, Leonard Cheatham,
Joseph Scales, (Henry Smith agent for Admn), William
Hill, John Dillard, Tax for 1814-1818, William
Spencer, P.R. Gilmer.

II:333-334 Inv SAMUEL M. COLE 13 Dec 1817 Ret Mar Ct
1818
10 horses, livestock, tobacco, grain, negros: Joe,
Moses, Joe Ross, Armstead, Andrew, Rachel, Venus,
Milly, Janny, Betsy, Nelly, Sindy, Polly, Sarah,
Henson, Amelia, Jackson, Davy, Charles, Billy,
Kitty, Will, Ned, Henry, Nelson, Ben, Charlotte,
Maria, Dennis, Tabby, Rachel, Phil, Major, Usley,
Cretty, Sandy, blacksmith tools, furniture
T:$15,696.57 by O. Redd, Joseph Bouldin, John Reamy.

II:334-335 Acct JAMES TAYLOR 12 Sept 1818 Ret Sept
Ct 1818
In acct with Elizabeth Taylor Admn.
Pd: Greensville Penn, Edward Staples, Robert Taylor,
John Redd, James Moore, Thomas Hill, John Hughes,
James Fulkerson, Joseph Rea, George Martin, William
Gray, Ruth Atkinson.

II:335-336 Inv JOHN HEFFLEFINGER 3 Nov 1818 Ret Dec
Ct 1818
Livestock, horse, furniture, no T.
By: Thomas East, Robert G. Payne, John Reamy.

II:337-338 Inv OVERTON REDD June Ct 1818
Furniture, horse, livestock, negros: Oba, Randal,
Clinton, Hannah, Nancy, Nelly, grain, no T. By
Thomas East, John East, Robert G. Payne.

II:338-339 Inv WILLIAM DRAPER 23 Apr 1818 Ret June

Ct 1818
Smith tools, plantation tools, furniture, negros:
Bob, Margaret, Jinny, Peggy, horses, bonds on:
Benjamin Davis, Thomas Wooten, W. H. Wooten, Joseph
Pace, Richard Bradberry, Asa Draper.
By: John Barksdale, Joseph Phifer, Michael McDonald.

II:340 Acct PETER LARRISON 6 July 1818 Ret July Ct
1818
By Peter Larrison Jr, Admn.
Cash of Mary Larrison, A. Norman, Polly Larrison,
James Larrison, P. Larrison.
Pd: James Larrison, D. Brown, D. Stone, W. Redd,
Joshua Lindsay.

II:340 Dower MARY JAMERSON now MARY MAYS 20 Dec 1817
Ret Jan Ct 1818
Land allotment: beginning at Richard Watson's line,
oak in Thomas Harbour's mountain tract, Thomas
Jamerson's corner, 130 ac including house.
By: Robert Anderson, James Moore, Thomas Harbour.

II:341 Acct of PHEBA DILLEN guardian of POLLY DILLEN
infant and legatee of HENRY and MARY DILLEN decd.
Mar Ct 1817

II:341-342 Inv THOMAS WILSON July Ct 1817
Negros: Old Sarah, Mourning and children, Arch,
Charlotee, Jack, Davy, Reuben, Rody, Milly, Sally,
Peter, furniture, livestock T:$4571.60 by Ely (x)
Bryant, Allen (x) Smith, Frank (x) Gilly.

II:342 Inv PETER LARRISON July Ct 1817
Furniture, Livestock T:58.12.3 by William Hewlett,
Richard Gilley, John Stratton.

II:343-344 Inv JOHN STAPLES 10 Apr 1817 Apr Ct 1817
Furniture, tobacco, Livestock, negros: Moses, Aggy,
Squire, Sandy, Billy, Daniel, Rachel, Eliza, Adam,
Charles, Pheba, Ned, Sopha, Snicha, Christine, Ader,
Roger, Sarah, Nancy, Lisha, Henry, Fontain, Mike,
Mary, Ester, Resiah, Polina, Burwell, Reubin,
Salern, Moses, Harrison, York, Gransvile, Slipha,
Samson. T:$15,266.23 by John Dillard, H. Hatcher,
William Spencer.

II:344 Dower ELIZABETH HEARD 10 Jan 1817 Ret Mar Ct
1817
Elizabeth Heard, the widow of William Heard, her
1/3rd on the waters of Town Creek being 188 ac with
house, 1/3 of 716 ac, also 46 ac of 167ac, also 50
ac on the said Creek part of 126ac.
By John Philpott, Samuel Philpott, Thomas Nunn.

II:344-345 Inv. GREENWOOD W. BOULDIN Sept Ct 1817

Furniture, Tobacco, horses T:$462.00 by Patrick H. Fontaine, John Reamy, Thomas R. Dandridge.

II:346 Sales est DANIEL SMITH 16 June 1820 Ret July Ct 1820
To; Green Trent, George Hairston, Polly Smith, Franky Smith, Elizabeth Robertson, Charles Hardy, John R. Salmon, Mark Bradbery. T: $344.41.

II:346 Inv SUSANA DILLEN Aug Ct 1820
Cash, corn, furniture T: $488.50 by John C. Traylor, James D. Marshall, William Dillen.

II:347-348 Acct HENRY LYNE 11 Aug 1820
Sept 1806: Lewis Franklin overseer, John France, John Redd, Thomas Dix & Co, James Meredith, John Benby, Charles Copland, John French, John Cox, John B. Trent, George Hairston, William Hunter, George Waller, William Mills, Charles Smith, John Smith, George Tucker, William Heath, P. H. Fontaine, P. R. Gilmer, Charles Hibbert, William Dillen, Greensville Penn, Thomas and William Bouldin, John Bailey, Rev. James Patterson, Thomas Bouldin, William Heath, Joseph Jones, John Salmon, Charles Fodrell, Thomas Starling, Henry Lyne.

II:348 Inv JOSEPH REA 27 Nov 1819 Ret Aug Ct 1820
Furniture, livestock, no T
By Robert Anderson, Alexander Moore, David Mullins.

II:349-350 Acct JOSEPH MARTIN Aug Ct 1820
Sept 1817 in acct with Joseph Martin, Adm
George King part of his legacy thru marriage with Susana Martin.
To: Samuel Armstead, P. H. Martin, Reuben Hughes, Lewis Martin rent and part sold.
Pd: Thomas Martin his part of property sold by Joseph Martin.

II:351-353 Sales HENRY LYNE 27 Feb Ret Aug Ct 1820
Peter Garland, William French, Thomas Starling, Stephen King, Peter Leak, William Shelton, Hezekiah Salmon, William Hunter, Russell Cox, John Bailey, John Ray, David Cousins, Jane Harris, Thomas Moore, Sam Hill, Thomas East, John Cox, John Christian, Joseph Jones, William Bouldin, John B. Trent, William F. Mills, George Waller, George Taylor, John Waller, Henry Lyne, Pines Allen, Lewis Franklin, John Redd, Robert Rowland, James McCulough, William Hurd, P. R. Gilmer, John Salmon, John Bailey, Joseph Alexander.

End of Will Book II.

WATER FEATURES- Henry County
```
Beaver Creek            14
Big Bull Run            17
Blackberry Crk          61
Buttram Town Crk        14
Buffalo Crk             19
Craddock Crk            14
Dols Crk                19
Fall Crk                43
Horsepature Crk         11;14
Leatherwood Crk         5;55;58
Marrowbone Crk          5;11;42;44;48
Middle Crk              43
Ramsey Crk              14
Redd Crk                14
Rock Run                14;66
Rockcastle Crk          14
Smith River             14;19;25;56
South Mayo River        90
Town Crk                92
Turkey Cock Crk         27
Turkey Pen Br           13
Warp Mtn Crk            14
White Falls             19
```

PLACE NAMES, ROADS
```
Ft. Patrick Henry        1
Goochland Store         10
Holston River           36
Powell's Valley 24;37
Richmond & Lynchburg Rd  50
Morgan Bryan Rd         14
Washington Iron Works    6
Western Country         36;62
```

VIRGINIA COUNTIES/CITIES
```
Albermarle Co           30
Amalia Co               76
Amherst Co              10;16;88
Bedford Co              1;27;30
Botetourt Co            88
Buckingham Co           16;18;36;42
Caroline Co             16
Cumberland Co           20
Franklin Co             20;23;29;46;72
Goochland Co            10
Henrico Co              23
Lynchburg               54;75
Mecklenburg Co          54;63;68
Montgomery Co           13;37;53
New London              38;42;43
Patrick Co              33;37;45;69
Pittsylvania Co         1;5;10;18;31;38;42;76
Petersburg              20
Prince Edward Co        42
Prince William Co       25
Richmond                16;54;88;89
Salem                   38
```

Other States

Broad River, S.C.	20
Charleston, S.C.	37
Dan River, N.C.	36
Hancock Co, GA	57;72;73
Kentucky	82
North Carolina	10;18;27;36;38
Rockingham Co. NC	90
Statesborough, S.C.	37
South Carolina	29;37;80
Tennessee	60;89
Wilks Co. GA	31

ABINGTON
  Henry 79
  William F. 61
ABNEY
  Abraham 35
  Nathaniel 35
ABSTON
  Mary 19
ACUFF
  John 41
ADAMS
  Daniel 39
  George 84
  Jacob 25
  Jacob Jr 28
  James 18
  Joseph 12*
  Luke 44;48;49;50;52;
    54;55;71;73;80;
    82(2);83
  Nancy 18
  Randal G. 89
  Randolph 50;70;78;82
  Richard 2
  Susannah 73;82
  Thomas 4
  William 11;38
  William P. 75;85;86
ADKINS
  Jesse 24
AENET
  Billy 80
AGEE
  Adler 70;79
  Charles 87
AIKEN
  Garland 5;11;18;23
  Nicholas 58
AISTROP
  Henry 54;63
AKIN
  Nicholas 79
  Tapley 83
AKINS
  Jane 58
ALEXANDER
  Boneparte 49
  Daniel Reamy 49
  Elizabeth 69
  J. 35; 36;38;50
  John 3;7;20;23;30;31
    43;44(2);46;47;48(2);
    52;54;79;80;82(3)
  Joseph 73(2);82;93
  Mary 49
  Reuben 63
  Robert 48(2);50;82
  Thomas 44
  Winney Jones 70
ALEXANDER & CO 88
ALLEN
  Darling 85;86;87
  Joseph 50;69;70
  Pines 85;87;88(2);89
  Robert 50;57;70;73;82;
    85;88;89
  Samuel 11(2)
  William 50*
ALLEY
  Nicholas 18;23
AMOS
  William 19
ANDERSON
  David 26
ANDERSON DAVID & CO 62
ANDERSON
  Peter 73
  Robert 44;46;48(2);
    55;73;78;80;81(2);
    82(2);83;92;93
ANGLIN
  Adrian 58
  Bhill 54

ANGLIN
  Phillip 2;5;54(2);71;
    79
ANNETT
  Samuel 31
ANTHONY
  Betsy 74
  Boling 17
  Christopher 17
  Elizabeth 17;70
  Jacob 74
  James 17;27;30(2);42
  Jane 52;72*;81
  Joseph 17*;17;25;27*;
    28;30*(2);40;42;44(2)
    70*;71;72;72*;74;74*;
    79;80;81;81*
  Joseph Jr 70
  Joseph Sr 10
  Josiah 74
  Judith 17
  Mark 17
  Micajah 17;30
  Rachel 17
  Samuel 70;74
  William 70;74
  Wineford 17
ARMSTEAD
  Samuel 89(2)
ARMSTRONG, Hugh 1(2)
  James 7(2); 21
ARNOLD
  Benjamin 33
  Elisha 69
  Elizabeth 23
  Sally 69
ARON
  George 84
ARS
  Mary 24
ASKIN
  Alexander 76
ATKINS
  Ann 13
  Robert 82
ATKINSON
  Elizabeth 60
  Isaiah 60;61;77
  Jesse 38;60*;61;79*
  Jobb 61
  Joseph 78
  Ruth 60(2);61;91
  Sally 60
  Sollaman 61
  Stephen 61
  William 61
AUSTIN
  Stephen 84
  William 84(2)
AYLETTE
  John 28

BAILEY (see Baley)
  J. 75
  John 27;50;56;89*;
    93(3)
  Joseph 82
  Martha 1
  Parks 73
BAIRD
  Samuel 12
BAKER
  Daniel 61
  Edward 11;18
  German 61;85
  James 25;29(2);31;
    34;36;39;61;74;75;
    80;84*
  James Jr 61;74;75
  James Sr 61*;71
  Jeremiah 61;74;75
  Robert 18
  Sally 61

BAKER
  Thomas 61
  Jemimah 61
BALEY
  James 33
  John 79
  Martha 1
BALTCHER
  Thomas 18
BANKS
  Dr. 73
  John D. 52
  William 33;73;82(2)
  William Dr. 78;86
BARBER
  Lucy 80
BARKER
  William 38
BARKSDALE
  Beverly 22
  Claband 22
  Dudley 22
  Henry 5;6;22*;86
  Henry Hickerson 22
  Hickerson 66
  John 22(2);25;46*;59;
    74;86;92
  Judith 22
  Sarah 22
  Thomas 1
BARKSDILL
  Henry 23;23*
BARNARDS
  28
BARNS
  Adam 1(2)
BARRETT
  Shadrack 28
BARRINGTON
  James 76
  Joseph 53;71;77;83;
    84
BARROW
  Susanah 69
BARSDEN
  John 32
BARTEE
  William 12
BARTON
  Thomas 44
  William 22;24
BASSETT
  Alexander 89
  Burwell 75;78*
  Nathaniel 34;38;43
  Nathaniel G. 85;87
  Polly 51
BATES
  John 18;23
BAUGH
  Daniel 19
BAYS
  Micajah 7
  William 59;84
BEARD
  Samuel 12
BECK
  Ann 46
  Anna 60
  Frederick 89
  John 46;60*;89*
  Mrs. 89
  Richard B. 84
  Robert 60;89
BEEN
  Rhody 45
  Robert 46

BELL
    Henry Col. 16
BENBY
    John 93
BENDER
    John 4(2)
BENDEVENTER
    Abraham 12
BETTY
    Abel 11*
BEUSER
    James 52
BINGTON
    Henry 74
BIRCHETT (see Burchett)
    Ann 63
    Nancy 68
    William 54;63;68;75
BITTING
    Anthony 10
BLACK
    Frederick 38
BLACKGROVE & CO 88
BLAGG
    John 1;4;6*;14*;28;
      32*
BLAIR
    Joseph 12;13
BLAKELY
    Thomas 52
BLAKEY & MAUPIN 15
BLAKY
    Agnes 17
BLANKENSHIP
    Iaham Jr 10
BLUFORD
    James 10
BOATMAN
    Agga 19(2)
BOHANNON
    Jeremiah 18;23
    John 1
    Joshua 1
BOLES
    John M. 51
BOLIN
    James Jr. 75
BOLLING
    Abe 16
    James 20
    Rebekah 24
    Samuel 16;17
    Sarah 24
BOOKER
    Richard 84
BOSTICK
    Abraham 38
BOTTETOURT
    John 33
BOULDIN
    Joseph Sr 89
    William 93(2)
    Alexander 55
    Christopher 37
    Fortune P. 74
    Green 44(2);66;74;75
    Greenwood 86*
    Greenwood W. 92*
    James Jr. 52
    Joseph 29;36;53;58;
      79;84;86;89;91
    Joseph E. 87
    Joseph Jr 63;66;67;85
    Thomas 54;85;93
    Thomas Jr 56
    Thomas Clark 70

BOULDIN
    William C. 60
BOULDIN & HUNTER 74
BOWEN & CO. 75
BOWLING
    John 83
    Joseph 28
    Thomas 44
BOWLS
    Joshua 5
    Sarah 5
BOWMAN
    William 3
BOYD
    Harrison 50
BRADBERRY
    James 59
    Richard 26;39*;41*;
      92
    Tabithia 41;59
    Mark 93
BRADBURY
    C. 90
    J. 90
    Maske 85
    Richard 26

BRADFORD
    Dr. 88
BRADLEY
    Mark 87
BRANDON
    Thomas 18;22;23
BRANHAM
    John 24
BRANNUM
    Barnabus 20
BRASHEAR
    Ann 1; 40
    Phillip 40*
BRASHEARS
    James 52
    Patsey 59
    Philip 27;48*

BRASHER
    James 82
    Nancy 82
    P. 82
    Philip 81*
    Philip Jr 82
    Robert 81;82
BREWER
    Nancy 85
    William 56;74*;79;88
BRIDGES
    David 10
BRISCOE
    Dr. 39
    John 2;10;20
BRITTON
    George 38
BROCK
    Allen 20
    John 20;20*
    Sally 20
    Sherad 20
BROOKS
    Phil 82

BROWN
    D. 92
    Janson 12
    John 21;38
    Ruffen 43
    Thomas 40;44
    William 19;21;35;
      43;56
BRYANT
    Ealy 59
    Eli 42(2)
    Elie 52
    Ely 92
    John 11
    Lewis 85;87
    Nelson 84
BUCK
    Judy 13
BUNDRAN
    Clabourne 87
BUNDRANT
    Jacob 87
BUNDREN
    Clabourne 85
    Jacob 85
BURCH
    John 4
    John Jr 57
    Sally 57
BURCHETT
    Ann 90
    Young 51
BURDET(T)
    William 15;16
BURGES
    David 77
BURGESS
    Davis 49;57;64
    John 49;50;53;57;57*;
      64
    Mary 57
    Mary A. 57
    Pendleton 53
BURGIS
    Davis 86
    John 40
    Pendleton 83
BURKS
    John 34
BURNETT
    Barna 52
    Edward 32
    Godfrey 77
    Jeremiah 24
    John 52
    Judea 60
BURNS
    Alexander 26
    Andrew 26
    Ann 24;26;57
    Charles Jr 26
    Charles Sr 26
    John 26
    Mary 3
    Samuel 26
    William 26
BURRIS
    J. 75
BURTON
    David 77
    Levy 56
BUTLOR
    Henry 30*
BUTTERWORTH 19

CORN
  Samuel 80

COTERILL
  Spencer 84

COUNES
  Phillip 81

COUSINS
  David 93

COWAN
  Robert 15;16

COWDEN
  James 9
  William 12

COX
  C.,Dr. 44
  Charles 35(2);53;81
  Francis 38;53;59*;65;
    80(2);83;88*
  John 9;12;22;25;26(2);
    28;31;32;35(2);35*;
    38;40;41;45;46;49(2);
    51(2);62;66;70;73;74;
    77;79;80;93(2)
  John C. 50;80
  John Jr 45
  Lainey 32
  Leanner 35
  Reubin 35
  Richard 83
  Rubin 35
  Russell 1;83(3);93
  Thomas 35
  Toliver 1
  Tunstall 81
  William 32*

CRAG
  Thomas 34

CRAGHILL
  William 28

CREASY
  John 45;50
  William 88

CRITZ
  Hamon 12;22;28;33(3)
  Hamon Jr 1
  Hamon Sr 2;26
  Jacob 33

CROUCH
  Jesse 75
  John 82
  Mary 68

CRUTHCHER
  Samuel 25;29;30;37

CRUTCHFIELD
  Samuel 13;36

CULVERSON
  Alexander 82

CUNNINGHAM
  Frances 34
  John 14;23*;54
  Thomas 29

CURD
  Richard 44

CUSON
  Thomas 53

CUSTER
  David 73;82;85;86;87

DABNEY
  Anny 9
  Frank 78
  John 38;39;41;42;49;
    54;71;79
  William 4*;9*

DANDRIDGE
  John 38
  N.W. 49(2);54;55;59;
    65;70;71;73;75;80;84;
    89(2)
  Nathaniel W. 48;54
  Thomas B. 84;89
  Thomas R. 93

DANIEL
  John 13

DARNELL
  Nickolas 6
  Susannah 21
  Thomas 21

DARNOLD
  Nicholas 28

DAVID
  Abraham 17
  Anna 17
  Elizabeth 17(2)
  Isaac 17
  John 40
  Jude 17
  Magdalene 17
  Mary 17
  Peter 17*;17(2)
  Phebe 17

DAVIS 37
  Ann 65(2)
  Benjamin 65;90;92
  Charles 65*;83*
  Elenor 65
  George 38
  Isaac 65
  Jane 58
  John 8;45;71*;76;79
  John Sr 57
  Joseph 84
  Joshua 65
  Lewis 90
  Luis 41
  Moses 65
  Peter 65
  Rachel 65
  Rebecca 58
  Thomas Blackburn 65

DAWSON
  Betsy 10
  Martha 10; 27
  Martin 10
  Susanah 10
  Thomas 10*

DEGRAFFENAUTER
  John 71

DELOZEAR
  Ann 57
  Asa 57
  Edward 57
  Edward Sr 57*
  Jesse 57
  Rhode 57

DENNY
  JaMES 3

DENT
  Benjamin 90
  John 90
  Shadrack 65;75*;90
  William 90

DEVIN
  James 53(2)
  John 77

DICKENS
  Richard 4

DICKENSON 4;12
  John 12
  Mary 6
  Thomas 37
  Thompson 6

DICKERSON
  Elizabeth 72
  Jemima 67
  John 8;9;22;52(2);67
  Josiah 72
  Robert 72'
  Thomas 48;49;67*
  Thompson 28;32
  Widow 72
  William 67;84

DIER
  Gilbert 84

DILLARD
  George 54;74;79;85;86;
    87
  J. 89
  James 20
  John 3;4;11;15;33(2);
    37;38;42;50;57;60;61;
    66;68;69;85;88;90;91;
    92
  John Jr 60;67;71;76
  John, Maj. 16
  John Jr. 79
  Martha 3
  Peter 60;88
  Peter H. 66
  Thomas Col. 79

DILLEN
  Benjamin 11;34;35;37;
    38
  Carter 40;45
  Dr. 74
  George 67
  Henry 40;40*;45*;78*;
    85*;92
  Henry Sr 40*
  James C. 40
  John 40
  Joseph Carter 58
  Joyce 58
  Littleberry 58;70;74
  Mary 40(2);78*;85*;
    92
  Patty 40
  Pheba 92
  Phebe 40
  Polly 92*
  Sally 85
  Sarah 40
  Susana 93*
  Susanah 38;40;44;58*
  Tabitha 67
  William 34*;35*;39*;
    40;45;48(2);54;56;70
    (2);74;78;79;80(2);
    81;82;89;93(2)
  William Sr 31*;38*;
    39*

DILLENDER
  Henry 82

DILLING
  Jessee 9

FOX
    James   18
FRANCE
    Daniel 1
    Elizabeth   1
    Hamon   1
    Henry   1;16
    John   1;1*;2;33;93
    Mary   1
    Peter   1;12;28;33
    Sarah   1
FRANCEY
    Susannah   27
FRANCIS
    Judy   64
    Polly   64
    Sally   64
    William 63*;77*;83
FRANKLIN
    Lewis   85;91;93
    Polly   55
FRANS
    John   33;39
FRAZIER
    Abraham 24;33
    Alexander   90
FRENCH
    Catherine S.   62
    John   62;93
    William 35;37;41;88;
        89;93
FULCHER
    GEorge 33
FULKERSON
    Frederick   2;3;18
    James   91

FUSON
    John   18;23

GAINES
    Thomas 89
GARDNER
    Samuel 14
    William 19
GAREN
    Lucy   38
GARLAND
    James   27;53;54
    P. 43;44;78
    Peter   44;48;50;55;69;
        72;75;77;78;80(2);
        81;82(2);83;90;93
GARNER
    Abel   47
    Elin   47
    John   47
    Obediah 47
    Sarah   47
    Thomas 47;47*;48*;
        58; 6*
    William 47
GARRETT 84
    Joseph 55
GATES
    John   25
GEAR
    John   90
GEARHART:GEARHEART
    Peter   9;48;49;54;79;
        82;83

GENTRY
    Watson 38
GIBSON
    Champane   4
    Cuzziah 4
    James   24
    Joel   4
    John   45;49
    Mary   4
    Thomas 4*;5*
GILL
    Nancy   61
GILLEY
    Charles 27
    Elizabeth   27
    Francis 27;27*;50;87
    George 27;59;83;40;50;
        52(2)
    Nancy   27
    Polly   59
    Richard 27;40;86;92
    Sibley 59
GILLIAM
    Deveraux   3
    Edward 3
    John B. 74
    Peter   4;10
GILLY
    Frank   92
GILMER
    George 54
    P. R.   78;85;93(2);91
    Peach R.   86
    Peachy R.   70;87
GOIN
    Elizabeth   74*
GOING
    Clabourn   45
    David   25
    Elizabeth   45(2)
    John   44*;45;45*
    Josiah 44;45
    Littleberry 45
    Nancy   44;45
    Shadrack   41
    Simeon 44;45
    Susannah   44;45
    Zachariah   44;45
    Zack.   29
    Zedekiah   44;45
GOLDEN
    Jacob   4*
    Mary   4
    William 4
GOLDSBY
    Daniel 5;36
GOODE
    Frances 4;15
    Jesse   4
    John   4*;4;14;14*;20;
        27*;34*;42*;35*
    Martha 4
    Nancy   4
    Sary   4
    Thomas 4
    William 44
GOODMAN
    Joseph 40
GOODWIN
    Joseph 1;32;35;38;42
    Polly   56   56
GOOLADAY
    Mr.   16

GOSSETT
    John   35
GOUD
    Joseph 67

GRAVELY
    Elinor 59;60
    Francis 60
    G. 84
    George 60;84;88
    Jabez   75;84
    Joseph 45;76'79;83;
        88(2);91
    Joseph Sr   68
    P. 84
    Peyton 88;91
    William 84(2)
GRAVES
    Betsey 28
    John   28;44
    Mary   28;44
    Miss   44
    Polley 28
    Sally   28
    T. 44
    Thomas 28;44;48;74;
        81;86
    William 27;28;30;36;
        44;44*;71*;75;85;87
    William Sr   28*
GRAY
    Elijah 78
    William 16;91
GRAYBILL
    Henry   72
GREEN
    Benjamin Capt. 16
    Myles   72;73
    Shadrack   52
GREENLEE
    James   51
GREER
    Ann 14
    Mary   14
    Mary Ann   14
    William 14;17
GREGORY
    J. 62
GRIFFIN
    Richard 76
GRIFFITH
    Benjamin   2;12
    Griffin 89
GRIGG
    James   76
GRIGGS
    Margaret   58
GRISIM
    John   4
GROGAN
    Henry   18;35
    John   32
GRYMES
    John   10
GUNN
    Elisha 50
GWILLIAM
    Lewis   28
GWINN
    Richard 20

HADON
Anthony D. 84

HAGGARD
James 19

HAGWOOD
Anderson 70

HAILE
Stephen 16

HAILEY
James Sr 77
Thomas 70;76

HAIRFIELD
David 88;89

HAIRSTON
Col. 18
Col. G. 32
George 5;6;10;15;16;22;
23;24;25;27;28;30;31;36;
38;39;41;42(3);44;46;
48(2);49;51;52;54;55;58;
59;60;67;69;70;71;72;73;
74;75;78;79;80;81;82;83;
84;87;89;90;93
George Jr 87
Hardin 75
Peter 3;6
Robert 54;60
Samuel 20
Sheriff 42

HALBERT
William 4;33

HALE
Bolling 73
William 54;66;73(2);
76;81;82
William Dr. 79;89

HALEY
John 19

HALL
Isham 12
Jesse 12
John 29;39
Johnathan 29
Mary 16
Million 3
Nathan 1;19;21;29
Randolph 29
Thomas Row 29
William 16
Sarah 29*

HAMBLETON
George 27
Thomas 15;34

HAMBRICK
Nancy 39

HAMILTON
Keziah 84

HAMPTON
John 38;42*;43
Lilyan 3*
Tabithia 43
William 38

HAMUSENDE
John 47

HANBY
Jonathan 26
William 75

HANCOCK
George 23
William 38

HANKINS
Gilbert 84
John 84
Leroy 84

HANKINS (contd)
William 89

HANKS
Moses 25

HANNAH
R. 42
Robert 41
William 32

HARBOUR
Abner 2*
David 2
Elisha 2
Esaias 3
Joel 3
John 71
Joyce 2
Moses 2
Sarah 71
Thomas 2;54(2);67;71
87(2);92

HARDMAN
Thomas 43

HARDY
Charles 85;87;93
Spencer 90

HARFIELD
David 53

HARRIS
Fanny O'Conner 62
George F. 38
James 9
Jane 93
John 38;81
Mary Ann 61
Moses 2*
Nathan 74
Nathaniel 89
Patsey 61
Peter F. 88
Wallis 62
Emalin 61

HARRISON
Benjamin 44;83
Benjamin Jr 42
Benjamin (W.B.) 43
George 91
James 76
Sally 43;44;80
William 43;56

HART
Andrew 32

HARTT
G. 1

HARTWELL
John 9

HASKINS
Daniel 28
Mary 54
William 12

HATCHER
Archibald 56*;67*
Archibald Jr 67;68
Charles 73
Eliza 54
Elizabeth 54
H. 86;92
Hubbard 74
William 67;68

HATCHETT
Timothy 16

HAWKINS EXORS. 35

HAWKINS
Mary 62

HAYNES
George 14;15;16;17
Henry 14*;14;15*;15;16;
16*
Henry Jr 16
John 14;15;16
Joshua 81
Parmenas Capt. 14;15;16
William 9;14;16

HAYS
John 60
Peter 60
Philip 60;77
Sarah 60
William 60*;78*

HEARD/HERD
Elizabeth 90;92*
George 9
Jane 14
Jesse 9;20;47;52;71*
John 4
Joseph 20
Justina 40
Nancy 47
Thomas 4
William 4;9;34;47;58;
74*;80;81;83;90*;92;
93
William Jr 14

HEATH
William 40

HEFFLEFINGER
George 65;87
Henry 55
Jacob 65
John 55;55*;64;65;65*;
72*;91*
Mary 65

HENDERSON
John 19;20;37;42;76

HENDRICK
Abraham 35

HENRY
Edward 41
John 36
Patrick 5;25

HENSLEY
Lewis 56
Nathan 87

HEREFORD
Dr. 74
John 87
William 63;65;68;77;
80;89
William Dr. 86;86*;55

HERNDON
Reubin 72
Richardson 55

HESTER
Samuel 63

HEWLETT see Hulet
Alford 21
Ann 21
Edward D. 57
Elizabeth 57
John 52
Martin 21
Nancy D. 57
Polly M. 57
Thomas 21;21*;23*

HEWLETT (cont)
  William 21;38;40;42;46;
  47;50;77;92

HIBBERT
  Charles 36;93

HICKENBOTTOM
  William 41

HICKEY
  Benjamin 14
  Cornelius 14
  Elijah 14
  James 14
  John 14;14*;21*
  Joseph 14
  Mary 14(2);15
  Michael 14
  Nancy 14

HICKS
  Elizabeth 5
  James 5*;12*;21*;31*
  Miles 5;16
  Nancy 5;21

HILL
  Hannah 1
  J. P. 61;78;89
  Johanah 1
  John P. 61;86
  John W. 91
  Mary 1
  Mr. 64
  Robert 1*;2;52*
  Sam 93
  Samuel 56;62;75;76*;78
  Thomas 52(2);54;69;91
  Thomas S. 71;85;87
  William 43;56;57;83;85;
  87(2);88;91
  Ruth 1
  Swinfield 1;4;11;17;
  18;23;
  Thomas 1;4;11
  Vilote 1

HIX
  Benjamin 31
  Nathaniel 30
  Polly 31;33

HOBARD
  Harrison 34

HOBSON
  Joseph 46;54;73

HODGES
  Aaron 9
  Abednegoe 9;12
  Amnijah 9
  Asa 9
  Isham 9*;12*;13*;72*
  Isham Jr 9
  Juda 9
  Keziah 9
  Martha 9
  Moses 9;12
  Nancy 9
  Robert 9;12;72
  Stephen 12
  William 9;12

HOFF
  Thomas 18

HOLCOMB
  Grymes/Grimes 7;15;23;
  90
  John 90*

HOLLAND
  Jonas M. 38;89
  Stephen 88
  Theadocia 60

HOLLANDSWORTH
  Susannah 21

HOLLOWAY
  Baines 9

HOLT
  Ambrose 8
  Barbara 8
  Elisha 8
  Fielding 36
  Francis 28
  Henry 24
  John 28
  Lucy 69
  Mildred 21;36
  Richard 21*;35*
  William 36;40;74;85;87

HOOKER
  Robert 22
  William 31

HOPKINS 21
  Richard 39
  Thomas 89(2)

HOPPER
  Betsy 56
  James 53*;56
  Joseph 42
  Mary 30
  Thomas 52

HOPSON see HOBSON
  Joseph 48;63;68;71;
  72;80;82(2);83

HORD
  John 24;25;26;29(2);
  45;49*;50*
  Mordecai 6;11;24;25;24;
  25*;26;29;30*;37*;80*
  Mary 25
  Ruth 50;51(2)
  S. 39
  Sally C. 50
  Stanwix 24;25;26;29(2);
  37;40;45;49;51(2)
  William 24;25;26;29(2);
  37;43;80;82
HORDS EXORS 37

HORNEY
  A. 55

HORTON
  W. 38

HOWARD
  James 48;72;79

HOWEL/HOWL
  George 32
  Parell 38

HUBBARD
  Benjamin 84
  Eusebus 8

HUDSPETH
  Robert 22;38
  William 7

HUFF
  John 10;18;23

HUGGINS
  William 16

HUGHES
  A. 33;53;71;72
  Abezah 43
  Abijah 82
  Ann 19
  Arch. 76;77
  Archelaus 2;6;12;15;53
  Beveridge 19
  Blackmore 18*;20*
  Blackmore Jr 18
  Col. 31;32;76
  Col. A. 16
  George 19
  Jemima 49
  John 18;19;78;91
  John Capt 85
  Letty 49
  Madison 77
  Madison R. 78
  Martha 19
  Moses 19
  Polly 89
  Rees(e) 42(2);50
  Reuben 53;77;89(2);86;
  93
  Rice 41
  Robert 19;38
  Sarah 53
  Terry 48;50;52(2);70*;
  72;80
  Thomas 19

HUGHES & HAIRSTON 33;36

HUHEY
  Elijah 51
  Nancy 51

HULET
  William 34

HUNT
  James 49*
  Owen 7

HUNTER
  A. 37
  Alexander 23;41;51(2);
  51*
  Dr. 73
  John 13;15;90
  Martha 51*
  Mary 13
  Mrs. 64
  Permelia 51
  Peter 51;80*
  Powhatan 51
  Robert 51;74
  Samuel 51
  Samuel H. 82
  Thomas 16
  William 4;13;14;17;27;
  42;43;93(2)

HURD
  William 93

HUTCHINSON
  Elizabeth 3
  Sarah 8

INES
  Henry 23

INGRAM
  James 11;20
  John 20;73

INNES
  Henry 10;19
  Hugh 28;34;8;9;12;20

IRVINE
  Samuel 54

ISAM
  William 19

ISHAM
  James 5
  Mary 5

JACKSON
  James 10
  Polly 37
  Thomas 89

JACOBS
  Susannah 64;83

JAMERSON see JAMISON
  John 71;80;82
  Mary 92*
  Samuel 90
  Thomas 81;87*;88;92

JAMES
  John 20
  Robert 74

JAMISON see JAMERSON
  Thomas 2;22;36;54(2);
    55;75
  William 12;20

JARVIS
  E. 37
  Mrs. 26

JASON
  Betsy 59

JENKINS
  James 87
  Lewis 9
  Mary 75;87
  Oliver 54;75;87
  Robert 72
  William 54*
  William R. 75*;87*

JENNINGS
  Samuel 43

JETT
  Capt. 80
  John 72
  Thomas 26;29;37;48;74;
    82

JINKINS
  Keah(Kiah) 85;87

JOHNSON 72
  James 17
  John 84
  Penelophy 17
  Samuel 1

JOHNSNTON
  James 49

JONES
  Ambrose 17;20;90
  Armstead 70
  Benjamin 39;48;53;55;
    58;68;70;72;75;76;80;
    81
  Buckner 52

JONES (contd)
  Delilah 70
  Elijah 22;23
  Elizabeth 7
  Fielding 70;88
  Frederick 30
  George 3
  Hannah 7
  Henry 7;45;70*
  Isaac 7*;9*
  John 17
  John Jr 3
  Joseph 17*;18*;22*;
    23*;55;70;72;83;93;
    84;87;88;89
  Lewis 53;70;77;83;89
  Mildred 70
  Milla 7
  Peter 70
  Rachel 7
  Robert 9;52
  Robert Jr 7
  Samuel 3*;70
  Sarah 7
  Susannah 7;23;70
  Thomas 2;4;9;22;23;38;
    38;39;80
  William 17;38;70
  Willis 70;77;84;88

JORDON
  Soloman 15;34

JOYCE
  Alexander 5;12;21;22;
    31;39
  Alexander Sr 26

KAYTON
  Jacob 32
KEATON
  Samuel 39
  William 33
  Zacheriah 33

KEEN/KEENE
  John 12;83

KEEPERS
  Thomas 6

KEERNLER
  Edward 48

KEETH
  Samuel 37

KELLEY/KELLY
  Andrew 9*
  David 72
  John 7;32;33;35;46;47
  Mason 47
  William 11

KELSO
  James 87

KEMP
  Samuel 39

KENDRICK
  Preston 67*
  Sarah 67

KERNAL
  John 64;83

KEY
  Crassey;Creassey 41;
    42;50;82
  George 41;41*;42*;43;
    49*;50*;74

KEY contd
  Isabel/Isabelah 41;42;
    43*;50;52
  Lucindy 41
  Martha Brasher 82
  Maryann 41
  Onah 41
  Rebeckah 41
  Sally 41
  Tandy 50
  Thomas 41

KIMBRO
  William 76

KING
  George 72;76;82;91;93
  Jeremiah 34
  John 27;44;53(2);56;
    60;70;76;88
  Joseph 15;34;52;90
  Molly 18
  Preacher 76
  Stephen 93
  Susana 93
  William 40*
  Zacheriah 4

KING & DYER 91

KINGTON
  Henry 75
  James 56
  John 88
  John Sr 85;87
  Joseph 85;87
  Reubin 85;87;88

KIRBY
  David 12
  John 12

KITCHEN
  Elizabeth 18
  John 18
  William 15

KOGER
  Henry 32
  Jacob 11*
  Joseph 20

LACK
  Abner 85
  Aleus 87

LACKEY
  Adam 19;20;24*
  John 11

LACY
  Polly 21
  Stephen 21

LAMB
  Richard 32
  Walter 32

LANE see Layne

LANEFORD
  Isham 38

LANES
  William 84

LANG
  Robert 12

LANGFORD
  Nancy 48

LANGFORD (contd)
Nicholas 3*
William 32

LANIER
Benjamile 18
Benjamin 48;84
D. 29;31
David 5;18;21;36;51;
56;82(2)
David Jr 73;83
David Sr 73
Elizabeth 18;57
James 82(2)
John 73
John H. 82
Lemuell 18*
Washington 18

LANKISTER
John 16

LANSFORD
Henry 38

LARGE
Robert 13

LARK
Dennis 72

LARRIMORE
Henry 48
James 44;54;81
William 48

LARRISON
James 92
Mary 92
P. 92
Peter 92*(2)
Peter Jr 92
Polly 92

LASUERE
Matel 82

LAW
Littleberry 12
Stephen 16

LAWLESS
Augustine 38
William 85

LAWRENCE/LAURENCE
Henry 49;67;75
James 84
Sarah 19
William 75;89

LAWSON
M. 31
Moorman 76
William 87

LAYNE/LANE
Dutton 38;45;48*;46*;
46;30;32;33
Dutton Jr 32
Dutton Sr 30
Elizabeth 46
Jeffery (Jeff) 46(2)
John 46
Mary 46
Molly 46
Nancy 46
Rhoda 46
Samuel 45;46;46*;47;
50;84
Sarah 45

LEAK/LEAKE
Ann 90
Elizabeth 90(2)
Hannah 77;85;87;90
John 73
Joseph 90
Josiah 85;87;90
Lucy 90
Nancy 90
Patsey 90
Peter 77;81;90;93(;93
Thomas 49
William 85;87;90

LEE
Lewis 39
R. 56
Stephen 9

LEMMONS
John 38

LEONARD
William 38

LESNEN
Martha 69

LESTER
Henry 10

LETCHER
William 7*

LEWIS
David 30
Edward 76*
James 32

LINDSAY
Caroline 16;36
Jacob 3*;16*;36(2);36*
James 16
John 16
Joshua 92
Patsey 36
Reubin 16
Sarah 16
Sarah Mrs. 16
William 16

LINDSEY
Mary 22

LITTRELL
Dinah 8

LOCKHART/LOCKHEART
David 29
Elizabeth 29
Martha 29
Patrick 9
Richard 29
Robert 29
Thomas 29(2);30;32*
William 29

LOGAN
Mary 26*

LONG
Jesse 73
Jesse Witt 67
Nancy 67
Nicholas 33
Reuben 55(2);56;74;88
William 79;83

LORTON
Robert 24;26;82;83

LOVELL
John 43;68;75

LOVELL (contd)
Markham 58
William 74;90

LOVING
Silvy 57

LOWE
Samuel 67
Thomas 2;18*

LUMPKIN
George 5;21

LYLE
Jonathan 75*
Richard 84

LYNE
Col. 81
Edmund 2;16;25;62(2)
H. 88
Henry 6;7;16;22;23;25
(2);29(2);34;38;41;51;
61*;62;93;93*(2)
Henry Col. 77*
John 62

LYON
Humberston 33
James 18;26;31;36(2)
James Sr 36
Stephen 24;26;33

MACKANGER
Aaron 19

MACKOY see Mc Coy
John 7

MAITLAND
Robert 42

MAJORS
James 9

MATLING
Jeams 20

MANAFEE see MENEFEE
William Sr 52

MANKIN
James 22

MANLEY
Richard 38

MANNEN
Davis 33
Samuel 28
William 28

MANNER
    Betsy 66

MANNING
    Samuel 20
    William 9

MARK
    Marey 10

MARR 16
    John 5;15;16;27;32;34*;
        36;38*;41*;42*;43*
    Susanah 27;38;41

MARRIDY
    Mary 65

MARSHALL
    Benjamin 69(2)
    Casandra 69
    Dennis 69
    James D. 93
    John 36;69
    Lewis 69
    Nancy 69
    Samuel 65;69*;72*;
        79;80;81;83

MARSTEN
    John 45

MARSTIS
    Elizabeth 79
    Elizabeth Jr 79
    Jacob 79
    James 78;79
    John 78*
    Thomas 78

MARTIN
    B. 44;72
    Brice 37;48;53;58;6;
        12;22;30;31;85;87;
        87*;89
    Brice Maj. 89
    Frankey 52
    G. 72
    Gen. 89
    George 78;91
    Hudson 78
    Hugh 7
    J. 72
    James 1
    James Sr. 74
    Jesse 53;77;85
    John 11;12;13;87
    Joseph 44(2);47;53(3);
        55;55*;56;58;71;71*;
        76;77;78;81;83;86;88;
        89(2);89*;90;93*;93
    Joseph Gen. 91
    Lewis 89;93
    P. H. 89;93
    Patrick 89
    Polly 53
    Stith 85;87
    Susannah 28;41;53;55*;
        89;91;93
    Thomas 89;93
    Unity 22
    William 1*;29;58;65;
        70*;84

MARTIN & GEARHEART 44

MASON
    David 55;73
    Robert 9;11

MASSHIRE
    Hawood 12

MASTERS
    John 41*

MASTIN
    James 84
    William 84

MATHEWS
    Elizabeth 51

MATTOX
    John 57;78;80;81

MAUPIN
    Jesse 29

MAUPIN & MEREDITH 74

MAUPON
    J. 90

MAXEY
    Jeremiah 15;16

MAY
    Caleb 38
    James 10;38
    Jonathan 38
    Joshua 38

MAYS
    Mary 92*

MAYZE
    Abraham 21
    David 21
    Gooding 21
    Henry 21;21*;22
    Liggin 21
    Littleberry 21
    Phebey 21(2)
    Sherwood 21

MC ALEXANDER
    William 20

MC BRIDE
    Patrick 34

MC COY
    John 7
    William 18;23

MC CRAW 42
    J. 75
    Jacob 15;86
    Samuel 85;87
    William 75

MC CULLOUGH
    Alexander 53;56;75;
        76;88
    James 53;88;93
    Susanah 68

MC DANIEL
    Isaac 25

MC DONALD
    Michael 59;92

MC GEHE
    Rina 23

MC GRUDER
    Blizard 41

MC GUFFORD
    Nathaniel 38

MC GUFFEY
    Henry 41

MC GUIRE
    Zacheriah 23*

MC HARG
    Alexander 6
    Mrs. 6

MC KEACKY
    James 52

MC KOWEN
    Archibald 87

MC MILLEN
    Abram 86
    John 84
    Stephen 86*
    William 84

MC REA
    John 38;41

MC ROBERTS 41
    William 37

MELTON
    James 6

MENEFEE
    William 17

MEREDITH
    Elijah 90
    Ka,es 71;93
    Juner/Junor 29;48;83;
        90

MILLER
    Jemima 3
    Mary 80
    Thomas 16
    Thomas Capt. 16
    William 16

MILLES
    Milley 48

MILLS
    Aaron 39;56
    David 69
    Sally 69
    William 27;39;50;56;
        89;93
    William F. 58;74;85;
        89;93

MILNER
    John 84
    Williamson 84

MINOR
    Elizabeth 45
    Huckeah 45

MINTER
    John 20;35;43;83
    Obediah 84

MITCHELL
    Agnes 19
    George 19
    John 19;21
    Richard 19;25
    Robert 19*;21*
    Thomas 38
    W. 42
    William 7;10;19;32;
        34;38(2);42(3);43;44;
        46;47;48;49;50;82(2);
        83

MOORE
    Abner 67

MOORE (contd).
Alexander 93
Ann 69.
Beddy 69
Benjamin 2;67;71
Charles 4
Collin 73
Eleck 69
Elizabeth 69;78
James 54;69;91;92
James Exors 54
Matilda 69
Mildred 2
Polly 61
Rhodham 38
Rod 13
Thomas 87;93(2)
William 4;32;48(2);
55*;69(2);69*;78*;
85;87

MORELAND
John 72

MORGAN
Anna 30
Bashaba 30
Haynes 5;39
John 30;30*
Littlebury 30
Lucy 30
Mary 30
William 30

MORMAN
Absalom 87

MORREY
James 24

MORRIS
Archibald 37;56
Benjamin 88
Dorothy 10
Far.. 37
George 37
Henry 85;87
Hugh R. 27
John 61;74;84;85(2);
87
Joseph 12;15;34;37*;
38*
Joseph R. 37
Judith 33;37
Lucy 37
Mary 37
Nancy 33
Samuel 12
Samuel C. 15;34;37;38
William 56

MORRISON
James 19
Nancy 19
Rebeckah 19

MORROW
Daniel 38
Thomas 21

MORTEN
Isaac 84

MORTEN & PETTY 91

MORTON
Isiah 84
John 84
W. T. 38

MOSLEY
Samuel 21

MOTTERBY
William 84

MOULDIN
Hezekiah 86

MULLINGS
Mathew 29
Jane 13
William 13

MULLINS
David 55;70;81;93
Henry G. 85;87

MURPHY
Arch. 40
Francis 59;90(2)
James 71;75;80;90
John 52
Leonard 85
Lydia 65

NANCE
Allen 68
Bird 68
Clement 68;70
Edmund 68
Isaac 68
Isham 68;74;75;76;80
J. 75
James 84
John 25;68
Joseph 68
Lessonla 68
Mary 70
Nancy 68(2)
Peyton 68
Reuben 35;48;53;56*;68;
68*;75*;76*
Reuben Saunders 68
Stephen 68;75
William 38;68;70

NASH
Marvel 4

NELSON
Sally 10
Thomas 10*

NEWMAN 3

NICHOLAS
Caroline Matilda 57
David 57
John 26;56*;57;81*
John Sr 56
Joseph 4
Thomas 56(3);79;85;88
Thomas Jr 57

NICHOLDSON
Ann 79*

NIGHT
Mary 8

NISLER
Hugh 48;80

NOE
Samuel 20

NORMAN
A. 92
Elizabeth 45
Sally 66
William 46;53;56;89

NORRIS
Jere. 38

NORTHCUTT
Capt. 83
Francis 71;76;90

NOWLAND
Richard 10*

NUMAN
Cairy 76

NUNN
Alexander 66
John A. 66;90
Joseph 66;67
Thomas 11;14;18;22;23(2);
31;39;46;61;66;67;73;
74;76;82(2);83;86*;
90;92
Thomas Sr 66*
William 73(2);80;82(2);
89

O'CONNER
Fanny 61;62

OAKES
Chandler 38
Charles 38
Hannah 77
Hezrkiah 56
James 32;42;56*;77*
James Jr 56
John 45*;49*
Josias 56
Laban 56

OFFICER
James 81
Thomas 85

OLDHAM 59
Elizabeth 60;88
John 45*;49*
Mrs. 71
William 88

OLIVER
Paige 39

ONEAL
Hugh 80*

OWEN
Obediah 84

OWENS
Charles 16
Christopher 15
John 74
Thomas 32

OZBOURN
Mrs. 75
Nancy 85;87

PACE
Joel 39;78;81
John 24;26;34;61;64;79;
80;83;86;39;42(2);43;
48
John Capt. 55
Joseph 92
Langston 78
Newsom 41;66;74
Polly 66
Robert 86
Thomas 54;73;78;82(3);
83
W. 23;24

PACE (contd)
    William 50;73
    William Jr 39
    William Sr 49

PACKWOOD
    Samuel 11

PALFREE
    John 5

PANNEL
    D.. 54

PARBERRY
    James 44(2)
    W.. 44

PARBURY
    Nancy 28

PARKER
    Samuel 3

PARKS
    Jesse 42

PARR
    Arthur 33
    Henry 22*;33*
    John 2;22;28;33
    John Jr 24;33(3)
    John Sr 33
    Milly 33

PARRISH
    John C. 53

PARSLEY
    John 4
    Thomas 34

PASLUR
    Isaiah 72

PATRICK
    Charles 27
    Hugh 35

PATTERSON
    Andrew 72
    James 53
    James Rev. 93
    Jarrott 16
    John 16
    Samuel 8;9

PATTERSON & SMITH 36

PAYNE
    Ab. 19
    Nancy 66
    R. 41
    Reuben 30;33;38(2);41;
      44;46;48;72;73;76;78;
      82;83;86;87;88
    Robert G. 48;88;91;86;87
    Wayland 76*

PEDIGO
    Robert 71

PEIRSON
    Meredith 79*

PENN
    A. 32
    Abraham 12;14;15;18;25;
      27;28;38;41
    G. Capt. 78
    George 29;52
    Greensville 91;93

PENN (contd)
    Patsy 52
    Thomas 88
    William 52

PERKINS
    Elizabeth 38
    HaRDIN 36
    M. 38
    Nicholas 36
    Peter 38
    Thomas 38
    William 87;88

PERRYMAN
    David 20
    Richard 9

PERSONS
    Joseph 13*

PETTY 72
    David 53;55
    Davis 77(2);84*;88;91

PHIFER
    Forest 90
    Joseph 29;90(2);92

PHILLIPS
    Elisha 73;87
    George 57
    Nelson 44

PHILPOTT 43;70;71
    Charles 39;41
    Charles T. 48;81
    John 34(2);38;39;51;
      70;71;92
    Samuel 51;74;80;90;92
    Sarah 68
    Zachariah 70;85;90

PHYFER
    Joseph 70

PILSON
    Richard 20;30
    Robert 19

PINKARD
    Charles 8;20
    Charlotte 8
    Elizabeth 8
    James 8
    Jane 8
    John 8*;9*
    Thomas 8

POLLARD
    Ann 19

POOL
    Micajah 1;7

POOR
    George 24
    Jeremaih 13

POPEJOY
    Edward 84

PORTER
    Mrs. 44

POSEY
    Thomas 34

POSTON
    Edward 69
    Soloman 90

POTTER
    Isaac 56

POUTAINCE
    Patrick 42

POWELL
    William 16

PRATHER
    Zachariah 12

PRATT
    Elizabeth 19

PRESTON
    Francis 37
    Hampton 33

PRICE
    John 9;12;38
    Joseph Showers 9
    William 56
    William B. 20

PRILLAMAN
    Daniel 58

PRUNTY
    Barney 88
    James 12
    Thomas 10;14;23(2)

PRYOR
    John 38

PUCKETT
    Thomas 13*

PULLIAM
    John 30
    Sally 56
    William 56

PYOTT
    Ebenezer 18;23

PYRTLE & ROWLAND 74

PYRTLE
    Arn. 81
    Ester 33
    John 22;33*;34;34*;38*
    John P. 38;71;81;81*;
      83;85;90
    Joseph 34;81
    Mary 34
    Nancy 34
    Samuel 34

QUARLES
    James 74
    John 50;76;78;80

RAKES
    Hugh 84

RAMEY
    John 31*
    Sanford 35

RAMSEY
    George 8
    James 8
    John 8;8*;9*
    Mary 8
    Randolph 8
    Thomas 8
    William 8;79

RANDALS
    John 30

ROYSTER (contd)
William 63
William J. 54;63

RUBELL
Owen 9

RUSSELL
John 3;22*;24*
Susannah 3

RUTHERFORD
Katherine 23

RYAN
Lucy 31
Obedience 5
Philip 3;5;73;82
William 8;9;12;17;20;34;
52

SALMON
Drury 39
George 85
Hezekiah 37;40;93
J. 44
John 5;6;10;15;25;26;
27;28;31;40;55;72;75;
86;89;93(2)
John Capt. 73
John Jr 56;58;65;85;91
John R. 90;93
John Sr 65;71;75;87
Thadius 55*;71*

SAMPSON
S. 10

SAMS
Elizabeth 3

SANDERS
Katherine 24

SANFORD
Sarah 68

SARRESON
Peter 46

SAUNDERS
Fleming 70;78
Peter 1;5;11;13;18;20;
23(2);31;37;52
Samuel 71

SAVAGE
James 72

SCALES
Anney 37
Anney Hardin 37
Bethenia 37(2)
Betsy 37
Constant 36
David 38
Henry 36;37
Joseph 32;36;36*;37*;91
Nancy 60
Nathaniel 37
Nicholas 36;89
P. P. 89
Peter 16;18
Peter D. 60
Peter Perkins 36
Robert 36
Susannah 37

SCOGGINS
Humphrey 2

SCOTT
J. 84
Thomas 16

SCRUGGS
Julius 1

SCURLOCK see SPURLOCK
James 33

SERRATE
John 88

SHACKLEFORD
Daniel 64;65;81;83
Henry 52*;53;64*;64;71*;
80*;81*;83*
James 64;65;81
Jane 77
John 52*;64;65;71;77*;
81;83
Luce 65
Mary 64;83
Samuel 64;65;71;81
Tabithia 68
William 58;64;65;81;83

SHARP
John 30;85;87
Robert 30
Samuel 33
William 22;28;30

SHAW
Josiah 27
Josias 18

SHEFFIELD
Leonard 85;87

SHELTON
Abigail 23
Azariah 23
Capt. 64
Cuthbert 22
Easop 23
Eliphaz 13;23;24;31;36;
76
Ezekiah 23
Francis 68
James 4;11;15*;15;16;
33;38*;39;56;68;76;
79*;88
Jeremiah 23
John 23;88
Liberty 23
Mary 23(2)
Molly 15
Mrs. 76
Nancy 15
Nathan 15;56;67;68;79*
Nathaniel 39
P. 56
Palatiah 23;33
Philepinea 15
Ralph 13;22(2);23;24;
24*;31;76*
Ralph Sr 23*
Roger 23
Sally 15
Samuel 38
Sarah 22
Wiatt 52
William 15;33;37;38;
43;83*;87*;93
Zebulon 1*
SHELTON & PANNEL 52

SHIELDS
James 71

SHIFLOT, Thomas 32

SHOATS
Sam. 32

SHOEMATE
Samuel 23;70
Toliver 84;88

SHORT.
Henry 24*

SIMMONS
Benjamin 73
Benjamin Jr 72
Sally Stovall 73

SIMMS
Ignatious 19;25

SIMPSON
Jesse 76

SINOOT
George W. 77

SLAUSE
Agnes 29

SMALL
Mathew 3;20

SMALLMAN
Guy 74
John 34

SMITH
A. 18
Allen 59;92
B. 49
Ben 75
Bird 16
Charles 58;66;70;90(;
93
Daniel 13;14;26;85*;
93*
Francis 35
Franky 93
Gideon 20
Guy 16
Henry 91
James 53
Joel 38
John 19;38;52(2);53*;
54*;55;79;83;91;93
Josiah 1;5;12
Moses 50
Peter 7;8;74;90
Polly 93
Robert 50;52
Sarah 53
Stephen 16;17;22;23
Thomas 1;12;16;50
Widow 28
William 54;71;85;87

SNELLL
Liza 69

SOLOMAN
Fanny 21
John 39
John Capt. 42

SOWAL
Joseph 1;4

SPANGLER
Daniel 18;23

SPEARS BROWN & CO 80

SPENCER EXORS 16
George Washington 11;42

SPENCER (contd)
James 2;3;6;9;11*;12*;
41;42*;43
James Jr 11
John 11;42
Margaret 11
Patty 51
William 11;12;42;75;78;
85;87(2);91;92
SPENCERS EXORS 37

ST. COX
William 27

STALLINGS
Jacob 15;16

STANDEFER 39
James 1;2
Luke 17
S. 42
William 18;22;23

STANLEY
Hannar Robert 13
Jesse 13
John 13
Judy 13
Mary 13
Moses 13
Richard 13
Robert 13
William 13;13*;15*;26*

STAPLES 31
Edward 75;91
Edward C. 85;86;87
George 90
John 16;18;21;25;34;38;
50;92*
Norman 85;87
Samuel 39

STARLING
Thomas 52;55;62;68;93(2)

STARMAN
Foxhall 38

STEPHENS/ STEVENS
Dudley 38;50
Soloman 25
William 13;38

STEWART
James 12;41
John 9
Thomas 52

STOCKTON
Richard 20
Robert 13;19;25;41;43;
49;50
Thomas 3;4

STOKES
Elizabeth Lumpkin 47
John 17;25;30;41;47*;
48*;75;80*
Polly 47
Thomas Haile 48
Ware 38
William 47

STONE 64
D. 92
Daniel 61(2)
Dosha 66
Elizabeth 36
Eusebus 29;34;36;39*;
74;74*

STONE (contd)
Jeremiah 61
John 11;45;54;55;56;70
Jonathan 53;77(2);88
Littleberry 90
Martha 41
Mary 45
Micajah 36;74
Polly 61
Richard 13;50;74
Stephen 66
Susannah 74
Thomas 11;36;66
Usebeous 45
William 36*;39*

STONE & STONE 91

STORM
Elizabeth 29
Nancy 29

STOVALL
Archibald 85;87
Brett 23
Dr. 77;90
Elizabeth 73;81
George 72;73
Joseph 52;73;81
L. P. 86
Landon P. 85;87
Pleasant 73
Polly 73
Ruth 73
Thomas 18;27;32*;38;
41;72*;73;81*

STRATTON
James 7
John 92

STUART
John 41

STULTZ
Gabriel 79*

SUMPTER
George 11
Gen. 80
Marget 34
William 38
Henry 26
SUTHERLAND
Alexander 23

SWANSON
John 20*
William 9;15;19;28

SWINGLE
Michael 38

SYMMS see SIMMS
Ignatious 90

TANKERSLEY
Richard 3;14

TARRENT
Carter 3
James 3;28
John 14
Larkin 3;28
Leonard 3*;4*
Leonard Sr 3
Mary 3
Rachel 3
Reuben 3
Richard 3
Samuel 20

TARRENT (contd)
Terry 3
Winifred 3

TATE
Caleb 72

TATUM
Edward 31
Jesse 26*
John 36

TAYLOR   80
Billy 80
Daniel 32
David 70
Elizabeth 78;91
G. 44
George 2;18;93
James 18;22;26;32;78*;
87;91*
John 36
Josias 81
Robert 91
W. A. 68
William 4;5;9;15;16;
18;77;85
William A. 58;87

TEDFORD
Margaret 29

TERRY
James 22*
John 22
Joseph 79;80
Patty 22
Peggy 22
Richard 22
William 52

THOMAS
A. 18
Charles 81

THOMAS DIX & CO 82;83;93

THOMASON
Amali 45
Anna 45
Elias 45
Flemon 45
Jany 45
Joseph 45
Phebe 45
Robert 45
Sarah 45
William 45*
Winey 45

THOMERSON
Adam 53
Arnold 76
Elias 83;90
Fleming 75
Peter 83;89;90

THOMPSON
James 24*
William 29

THRELKELD
Thomas 20

THURSTON
John 46*; 49*
William F. 49

TITTLE
Anthony 1

TOOMS
William 76

TOWLIN
Joseph 65

TOWNSEND
Joshua 8

TRAHERN
John 68;73;82
Joseph 73
Susannah 63;68

TRAYLOR
John C. 61;89;91;93

TRENT
D. 56
Dr. 56;74
Green 93
John 54;75
John B. 62;70;76;78;85;
93(2);55(2)
John H. 56

TRENT & CO 36

TROUP
Jacob 9*; 10
Mary 10

TUCKER
George 89;93

TUNSTALL
Col. 11;18
Peyton Randolph 6
Thomas Barker 6
William 3;5;6;28;32;42

TURLEY
Leonard 7
Peter 7*;9*
Samuel 7
Sarah 7
William 7

TURNER
Ann 13
Elizabeth 13
Exoney 13
Frances 20
Francis 24
Izrareal 1*
Jeremiah 13
John 1;13;15;59;74
Joseph 50
Josiah 13;50;74;90
Larkin 13;26
Mary 13;59
Milley 41
Nancy 59
Richard 52
Shadrack 13*
Shors 90
William 1;13;15;26;31;
34;37;38;50;70

TURPIN
James 7*
Margaret 7;10

VAMDERGRIFF
Leonard 2

VAUGHN
Caty 58
Elizabeth 58
Martha 58

VENABLE 31
R. H. 41
Richard 41

VENABLE (contd)
William N. 37

VERELL
John 46

VERNON
Nancy 33
Thomas33;35

WADE
Bartlett 6;45;74
James 88
John 74

WAGNON
John 5

WALKER
Joel 7
Sally 80
Sarah 27

WALLER
Ann 82*
Carr 53;77;80;86;91
Dabney 77;86
E. 75
Edmund 86;89;91*
Elizabeth 53;89
George 2;10;25;26;29;
31;45;74*;75;75*;78;
81;82;86;86*;87;93(2)
George Jr 41;82;85;72
John 49;54;55;56;67;
73'76'78'79;82(2);85;
86;87;83;93
John Capt. 85
Maria 89*
Martha 52*;53*(2);77*
86*
Sarah 89
Sarah Matilda 53
Susannah 53
William 86

WALLER & PETTY 91

WALLING
Elisha   2

WALTON
John 37

WARE
William 84

WARREN   WARRIN
Jesse 84(2)
Carr 53
George 84
Jane 47
William 71

WARWICK
Jacob 25

WASH
John 24;42;46;48(2);
80;82;83(2)

WASHINGTON
Ann 58
George 58
Soloman 58

WATKINS
Edward 71(2)
Eli 54(2)
Jarrol 20

WATSON
Alexander 12
David 58
Dr. 38
Edey 12
Elizabeth 12
James 12
John 12*;15;35*;36;58
Martha 12
Michael 57*;83*
Richard 56;92
Robert 58
Samuel 58
Sarah 22
Stinson 76;84
William 32

WATTS 28
Mary 6
Richard 6
Thomas 11*

WEATHERFORD
Benjamin 52
David 42*;51*;52*
Harden 52(2)
Joseph 52
Judea 52(2)
Judith 52
Mary 52

WEAVER
J. 44
John 36;54;56;66;77;81
Joseph C. 66
Zebedu 56

WEBB
Elizabeth 3;79*;80*
John 3
Lucy 3
Martin 3
Merry 3;28;39;79*
Merry Sr 2*;6
Samuel 8
Silvanus 1*
Morris 10

WEEKS
Elizabeth Stovall 73
John 72;73

WELCH
Richard 39

WELLS
Barna 53;67;72;76;77;
84;88;89
Barnaby 48
John 5;6;28;45;48*;67
Judith 48
Mathew 48

WEST
William 41

WHITLOCK
Betsy 66
William 19

WHITTELLS
William 17

WILCOX
Edmond 16

WILKERSON
John 52

WILLIAM & WORTHAM 72

WILLIAMS 81

WILLIAMS 80
    Abraham 89
    Col. 10;11;23
    Elizabeth 35
    Garrett 88
    Garrot 81
    James 35;43
    John 35;35*;43*
    Joseph 55;73;82
    Parmenas 46
    Robert 22;26;34
    Salley 18
    Silas 35;43
    Thomas 73;83;82(2)
    William 22;35

WILLIS
    Abel 49
    William 70

WILLS
    John 80;85;87
    John Sr 79

WILSON
    Aaron 52;59
    Betsey 69
    Daneil 43;86
    Elizabeth 33
    Ellis 84
    James 33*;34*;59;79;
    James Sr 1*
    John 38;41;52;59;79
    John Sr 52
    Martha 1
    Moses 1;27;52;59
    Nancy 59
    R. 73
    Sally 33
    Thomas 1;52(2);59;59*;
     92*

WINSTEAD
    William 30

WINSTON
    Edmond 10;16;27;36
    Patsey 80

WITT
    David 54*(2);67(2);67*;
     71*(2);74*
    Jesse 38;55;55*;56*;67*;
     70*;73;73*
    Joel 55;67;73;74
    John 54;67;71;74
    Joseph 67
    Martha 55*;67
    Sarah 54;67;71
    Widow 54
    William 74

WOOD
    Hugh 7;11
    John 7
    Robert 13
    William 41*

WOODALL
    Daniel 84
    James 84;88
    Jane 77
    Nathan 77

WOODING
    Robert 52

WOODS
    Richard 89
    Robert 74
    William 25

WOODSON
    Benjamin 69
    M. 42
    Shadrack 9

WORHAM
    Charles 83
    Daniel 46;50

WOOTEN
    Jane 85
    Thomas 92
    Thomas J. 87
    W. H. 92
    William H. 85;87;87*

WRIGHT
    David 3

WYATT
    Vincent 58;76

WORSHAM
    John 80;82

WORTHAM
    Robert 89

YANCY
    Charles 63
    Rebecca 54;63

YOUNG
    Comfort 38
    E. 18
    James 17

ZACHARY
    John 58*;80

www.ingramcontent.com/pod-product-compliance
Lightning Source LLC
Chambersburg PA
CBHW021835020426
42334CB00014B/639